Lessons Learned
from Public Workforce
Program Experiments

Lessons Learned from Public Workforce Program Experiments

Stephen A. Wandner
Editor

2017

WE *focus*
series

W.E. Upjohn Institute for Employment Research
Kalamazoo, Michigan

Library of Congress Cataloging-in-Publication Data

Names: Wandner, Stephen A., editor.
Title: Lessons learned from public workforce program experiments / Stephen A.
   Wandner, editor.
Description: Kalamazoo, Michigan : W.E. Upjohn Institute for Employment
   Research, 2017. | Series: WE focus series | Includes index.
Identifiers: LCCN 2017044711 | ISBN 9780880996303 (pbk. : alk. paper) | ISBN
   0880996307 (pbk. : alk. paper)
Subjects: LCSH: Public services employment—United States. | Manpower policy—
   United States. | Unemployment—United States.
Classification: LCC HD5713.6.U54 L47 2017 | DDC 331.12/0420973—dc23 LC
   record available at https://lccn.loc.gov/2017044711

The facts presented in this study and the observations and viewpoints expressed are
the sole responsibility of the authors. They do not necessarily represent positions of
the W.E. Upjohn Institute for Employment Research.

Cover design by Carol A.S. Derks.
Index prepared by Diane Worden.
Printed in the United States of America.
Printed on recycled paper.

Contents

Acknowledgments

The chapters in this book were first presented as papers written for the November 2015 annual meeting of the Association for Public Policy and Management. The papers were revised based on the excellent comments from the session discussant, Burt Barnow. The revised papers also responded to questions and comments from the audience at the APPAM session.

The most important contribution to this book comes from the authors, all of whom have worked on designing and evaluating workforce program experiments for many years. They share a common belief in the importance of using experimental methods to evaluate existing workforce programs and developing new approaches and programs to improve the public workforce system.

—Stephen A. Wandner

Chapter 1

Introduction

Stephen A. Wandner
W.E. Upjohn Institute and Urban Institute

This book presents an analysis of the lessons learned from public workforce experiments that have been conducted and evaluated in the United States. The U.S. Department of Labor (USDOL) has sponsored a large number of these experiments over several decades, and some of them have resulted in significant public workforce program and policy improvements. The USDOL has been a leader in making use of rigorous evaluations of existing workforce programs and in the development of new public workforce program options.[1]

These experimental evaluations of public workforce programs have included evaluations of training programs—the Job Training Partnership Act (JTPA) and the Workforce Investment Act (WIA)—and of the Job Corps. In the past, experimental evaluations have had an impact on public workforce policy. One example is an enormous cut in funding of the JTPA Youth program in 1995 following negative findings from the JTPA evaluation.[2] Another is the expansion of the Job Corps program at the beginning of the George W. Bush administration in response to a favorable evaluation of the program, despite an initial impulse to cut the program because of its high cost per participant.

Experimental methods have been widely used to develop new approaches to help dislocated workers return to work. One major effort was a series of unemployment insurance (UI) experiments that were conducted in the 1980s and 1990s to test new or improved reemployment approaches. Two sets of experiments resulted in the enactment of federal legislation in 1993: 1) a targeted, early-intervention job search assistance program known as Worker Profiling and Reemployment Services and 2) a self-employment assistance program for

1

UI recipients called, simply, Self-Employment Assistance (Wandner 2010). More recently, experimental evaluations of a UI work-search eligibility review and reemployment services program (Reemployment and Eligibility Assessment, or REA) has helped to increase funding for this program and encouraged the Obama administration to expand and restructure it as the recent Reemployment Services and Eligibility Assessment (RESEA) program. The experimental evaluation of public workforce programs has been a major component of all U.S. experiments over the past 50 years. For example, Greenberg, Shroder, and Onstott (2004) studied 293 social experiment interventions completed between 1962 and 1996. They found that at least 186 of the interventions, or 63 percent, could be categorized as public workforce experiments: job search assistance (33 interventions), work experience/on-the-job training (32), case management (32), counseling (23), wage subsidies (14), other employment services (13), job clubs (12), reemployment bonuses (10), job placement services (7), incentive bonuses to participate in education/training (5), child care for employment (4), and employer tax credits (1).[3] In the period since 1996, the number and diversity of social experiments has increased significantly, as has the percentage of experiments conducted outside the United States.[4]

Interest in evidence-based policy increased during the Barack Obama administration, especially the use of rigorous research and evaluation methods and randomized controlled trials (RCTs). Early on, the White House reserved funding for experiments and had federal agencies compete for these funds. The White House also issued guidance regarding evidence-based public policy and rigorous evaluations. More recently, the White House has encouraged small and large improvements in ongoing federal programs based on the results of low-cost experiments that used behavioral science methods. Specifically, in 2014 the Obama administration established the Social and Behavioral Sciences Team to build behavioral science findings into federal policy decision making. The cross-agency team was to be overseen by the White House Office of Science and Technology

Policy, with responsibility for translating findings and methods from the social and behavioral sciences into improvements to federal policies and programs.

A number of federal agencies, including USDOL, have funded behavioral economics experiments. One ongoing USDOL-funded project, the Michigan Reemployment and Eligibility Assessment Experiment, is discussed below in separate chapters by Randall W. Eberts and Christopher J. O'Leary. The Michigan experiment has made small changes to program outreach that have succeeded in having more unemployed workers participate in job search assistance programs. These types of incremental improvements to governmental programs are popularly known as "nudges," based on a book of that title (Thaler and Sunstein 2009).

Interest in improving governmental programs by learning from rigorous evaluations has in the past been bipartisan and widespread. In March 2016, Congress established the Commission on Evidence-Based Policymaking, with cosponsorship from Speaker Paul Ryan (R-WI) and Senator Patti Murray (D-WA). The commission is chaired by Katharine G. Abraham of the University of Maryland and Ron Haskins of the Brookings Institution. The commission's charge is to make recommendations about how administrative data can be made more accessible to researchers for policy evaluation purposes as well as to make recommendations on how rigorous evaluations can be made more integral to the ongoing operations of federal programs. A central task of the commission is the development of a plan for the establishment of an administrative data clearinghouse to support these program evaluation goals. The 15 commission members, appointed by the president, the House, and the Senate, have 15 months to issue a final report once membership is complete.

This book consists of four chapters. Their principal authors— Eberts, O'Leary, Irma Perez-Johnson, and Jacob Benus—have extensive experience in designing, implementing, and evaluating a substantial number of USDOL experiments. Conducting experiments tends to be time consuming and expensive, and successfully implementing experiments is complicated. Because there was increasing interest in carrying out rigorous evaluations, the authors decided that presenting issues and lessons learned in the successful completion of these projects would be instructive to researchers and public policy analysts. Early versions of the chapters that make up this volume were presented at the November 2015 meeting of the Association for Public Policy Analysis and Management, as indicated in the acknowledgments.

LESSONS LEARNED FROM PUBLIC WORKFORCE EXPERIMENTS

This book presents some key lessons learned from public workforce RCTs, covering both the evaluations of existing programs and the development of new interventions. Among the topics covered are the following:

Securing Funding

The Department of Labor has concluded that programs should be rigorously evaluated on a regular basis, and it has considered establishing a periodic evaluation schedule, such as evaluating major programs every five years. Generally, however, there has been insufficient funding to achieve this target. The funding shortage has become more acute in recent years because of a decline in funding for public workforce research in the USDOL budget. Yet there has been increased concern that public policy be evidence based, suggesting the need for substantial increases in evaluation funding.

Because of interest in using behavioral science research to improve programs, a number of federal agencies have provided funding for nudge projects. It is easier for the agencies to provide this funding since the cost of nudge RCTs tends to be much lower than that of other experiments, both because the interventions themselves have minimal costs and because they tend to be evaluated with administrative data rather than with more costly participant surveys.

Securing Participating States or Localities

State workforce agencies are primarily operational organizations for the delivery of public workforce services. State workforce agencies and their local American Job Centers often do not see the need for or the direct benefit from research and evaluation of their operational effectiveness and efficiency. As a result, these research and evaluation activities frequently are met with limited enthusiasm and given low priority. Social experiments tend to be implemented in the small number of states that are most interested in learning how to improve their programs using rigorous evaluations. Indeed, Greenberg, Shroder, and Onstott (2004) find that, between 1962 and 1996, 54 percent of all experimental interventions were concentrated in nine states.[5]

State participation in experiments can be voluntary or "recruited." If the combination of participating states need not be representative of the country as a whole, then researchers can rely solely on volunteers. But if a representative sample of states is sought, then states have to be recruited so that they are representative geographically and demographically. For example, all of the UI experiments made use of state volunteers and ran competitions for some of the experiments when there was an excess of expected volunteers. Similarly, for the Individual Training Account Experiment, USDOL solicited volunteer Workforce Investment Boards to participate. By contrast, the Job Corps and JTPA/WIA experimental evaluations were based on randomly assigned individuals or local offices, and each of these evaluations experienced participation problems.

States and local areas have traditionally had the option to participate or not in research and evaluation projects. Even though the major public workforce programs provide grants to states to operate, participating in these projects could be a condition of receiving grants. However, neither the Workforce Innovation and Opportunity Act (and its predecessor statute, the Workforce Investment Act) nor the Wagner-Peyser Act requires participation in federally funded research and evaluation projects, although the Workforce Innovation and Opportunity Act encourages states to conduct their own research and evaluations.[6] By contrast, the Job Corps statute does require participation. A similar problem involves the UI program. Section 303(a)(6) of the Social Security Act requires states to provide such reports as the secretary of labor may request, and these requests could include UI wage records that are used to assess the outcomes of many evaluations. Nonetheless, it has often been difficult to obtain state UI wage records to estimate the impact of a program or an intervention. In 2012, USDOL issued a UI program letter to try to assure that wage records would be made available by states in accordance with Section 303(1)(6) (USDOL 2012). The Department of Labor has also worked around state objections to providing UI wage records for federal evaluation by using the National Directory of New Hires.

Monitoring Experiments

The training of state and local office staff as well as the close monitoring of the operation of experiments have been critical to maintaining the fidelity and integrity of an experiment's design. It is easy for staff to stray from project procedures over time, and new staff must be trained over the life of the project.

It is helpful to have a number of monitors in the field. For the UI experiments, monitoring was conducted by the research contractor, USDOL staff, and state staff. The result of this three-level monitoring was the ability to maintain the integrity of the projects. For example, the Washington Self-Employment Assistance Experiment provided Self-Employment Assistance lump-sum payments averaging $4,225. State project monitors detected that a project staff member had approved payment to several project participants before the participants had met all of the criteria for payment, and the payments were not made. This was fortunate, because when the General Accounting

Office (as it was still called in the early 1990s) later conducted a 100 percent audit of all 451 payments made by the project, they found that all payments were made in accordance with project procedures.

By contrast, for a state-funded Illinois Reemployment Bonus experiment, monitoring was minimal, and conditions changed during the operation of the project. It was only after the publication of the project evaluation report that the integrity of the project was called into question, resulting in federal reemployment bonus experiments to verify the Illinois evaluation results.

Design, Implementation, and Evaluation Issues

There are a number of procedural issues discussed in this book, including whether or not an experiment will include a control group, random-assignment problems, and design considerations. The implementation and evaluation of experiments is a complex process. Greenberg, Shroder, and Onstott (2004) report that until 1996 the concentration of experience in conducting experiments in the United States resulted in a large percentage of the experiments being conducted by the so-called Big Three experimental evaluators: Mathematica Policy Research, Abt Associates, and Manpower Demonstration Research Corporation (MDRC). These three research and evaluation firms continue to be important, but expertise and experience have spread widely, and many other research institutions conduct and evaluate experiments, including IMPAQ International and the W.E. Upjohn Institute for Employment Research, both of which are represented among the authors of this book.

The design and evaluation process has a direct impact on the cost of experiments. The experiments discussed in this book vary in cost from under $100,000 (e.g., the Work First Experiment) to over $10 million (e.g., the WIA Gold Standard Evaluation). The cost of experiments is of critical importance in a world with stagnant or declining funding for research and evaluation. Future emphasis is likely to be placed on finding low-cost experiments, including nudge-type experiments.

Learning from and Using Results

Conducting experiments only makes a great deal of sense if they can influence public workforce programs and public policy. We will see in this book that experiments frequently have major impacts. For example, the JTPA evaluation resulted in temporary reductions in the JTPA Youth program while USDOL looked for better ways to administer youth employment programs. The initial REA evaluations resulted in restructuring and expanding funding for eligibility reviews and reemployment services. Demonstration projects can result in changing existing programs or creating new ones. Examples of the latter are the federal law creating the Worker Profiling and Reemployment Services program, based on a New Jersey UI experiment, and the Self-Employment Assistance program, based on the Massachusetts Self-Employment Assistance Experiment.

SUMMARY OF THE FOUR CHAPTERS

This book presents the design, policy, and administrative lessons learned from a series of experiments sponsored by the U.S. Department of Labor. The experiments include the small and inexpensive Kalamazoo Work First Experiment, which offers lessons learned for developing future low-cost, effective public workforce experiments. A series of reemployment bonus experiments offer a new policy initiative that has the potential to be cost effective if properly targeted. The Individual Training Account experiment helped to guide the design of training vouchers. Finally, the Nevada Reemployment and Eligibility Assessment Experiment, as well as two previous REA evaluations, have confirmed what has been learned from earlier experiments conducted in New Jersey; the District of Columbia; Florida; and Charleston, South Carolina; and this experiment reaffirms the need to provide reemployment services to UI recipients at the same time as conducting eligibility reviews.

Irma Perez-Johnson, Annalisa Mastri, and Samia Amin of Mathematica Policy Research draw on Mathematica's experiences in designing and implementing demonstration studies for the U.S. Department of Labor to discuss how "on the ground" realities shape study design, implementation, and results. They recognize that when designing pilot programs, study teams are faced with the need to balance innovation with practicality, and analytical rigor with feasibility. They draw on lessons from the Individual Training Account Experiment, the Self-Employment Training Demonstration, and the Workforce Investment Act Adult and Dislocated Worker Programs Gold Standard Evaluation, all conducted by Mathematica, to discuss the kinds of decisions and important issues that policymakers and researchers commonly negotiate, and how these can shape the design, implementation, and results of demonstration studies.

Randall W. Eberts of the W.E. Upjohn Institute for Employment Research writes about small, inexpensive experiments—both the recent effort to implement and use behavioral economics experiments to develop public policy, and an inexpensive Work First Experiment that demonstrates how low-cost public workforce experiments can be conducted. Reviewing the findings of the Work First Experiment, he discusses factors that can make local public workforce offices both more effective and more efficient in operating experiments.

Jacob Benus of IMPAQ International writes about the impact of the Reemployment and Eligibility Assessment Initiative and three REA evaluations that include quasi-experimental and experimental designs. He describes a series of research projects conducted by IMPAQ in four states; the projects find evidence that the REA program is effective in reducing UI duration and in generating savings for the UI Trust Fund (Poe-Yamagata et al. 2011). Because the evaluation of the Nevada program generated substantially larger impacts than the evaluations of the other three states' programs, the Nevada REA program study was extended to see whether it would confirm the initial Nevada findings. The results (Michaelides et al. 2012) do indeed confirm the earlier results—the Nevada REA program was highly effective in assisting claimants to exit the UI program sooner than they would have in the absence of the program. Based on these results, the study concluded that the combination of eligibility reviews and reemployment services is an effective model for reducing UI duration and assisting UI claimants in returning to productive employment.

Christopher J. O'Leary of the Upjohn Institute reviews the outcomes of a wide variety of workforce program field experiments, conducted mostly for the U.S. Department of Labor. Specifically, he reviews the results of the following: reemployment bonus experiments conducted in Illinois, New Jersey, Pennsylvania, and Washington; UI work test and job search assistance experiments conducted in Maryland, Washington, and Charleston, South Carolina; benefits rights interview experiments conducted in Massachusetts, Virginia, and Michigan; targeted job search assistance experiments conducted in New Jersey, the District of Columbia, Florida, and Kentucky; and employer incentive experiments conducted in Illinois, Washington, Massachusetts, Pennsylvania, Iowa, Oregon, and Dayton, Ohio. One of the studies he discusses is the Michigan Reemployment and Eligibility Assessment Nudge experiment.

This book presents an overview of a large number of workforce RCT demonstrations and evaluations that have been conducted over the past 35 years. It describes what was done and how these experiments have contributed to public policy, including the enactment of new legislation and the improvement of ongoing programs. It also presents the methods that have been used to ensure that these RCT studies are successful and that enable these studies to be conducted in a cost-effective manner. Taken together, the chapters of this book attempt to form a guide for conducting successful RCT studies in the future.

Notes

1. RCT experiments have been invaluable from a public-policy perspective in providing research and evaluations that are able to affect public policy, but they also have limitations. See Rothstein and von Wachter (forthcoming).
2. The decline in Youth grants to states was from $1.497 billion in 1994 to $311 million in 1995.
3. Other categories of interventions included education, income transfers, tax system, health, and electricity.
4. See David Greenberg and Mark Shroder's periodic online publication, *Randomized Social Experiments eJournal*, now in its ninth volume, generally published weekly.
5. The states and the number of interventions tested in each state were as follows: New York, 27; California, 26; Illinois, 19; Pennsylvania, 19; Ohio, 16; Florida, 13; Massachusetts, 13; Texas, 13; and Washington, 13.
6. Workforce Innovation and Opportunity Act, Section 169.

References

Greenberg, David, Mark Shroder, and Matthew Onstott. 2004. "The Social Experiment Market." In *The Digest of Social Experiments*, David Greenberg and Mark Shroder, eds. Washington, DC: Urban Institute Press, pp. 459–472.

Michaelides, Marios, Eileen Poe-Yamagata, Jacob Benus, and Dharmendra Tirumalasetti. 2012. *Impact of the Reemployment and Eligibility Assessment (REA) Initiative in Nevada.* Columbia, MD: Impaq International. http://www.impaqint.com/sites/default/files/project-reports/ETAOP_2012_08_REA_Nevada_Follow_up_Report.pdf (accessed March 27, 2017).

Poe-Yamagata, Eileen, Jacob Benus, Nicholas Bill, Hugh Carrington, Marios Michaelides, and Ted Shen. 2011. *Impact of the Reemployment and Eligibility Assessment (REA) Initiative.* Final Report to Congress. Columbia, MD: Impaq International.

Rothstein, Jesse, and Till von Wachter. Forthcoming. "Social Experiments in the Labor Market." In *Handbook of Field Experiments*, Abhijit Banerjee and Esther Duflo, eds. Amsterdam: Elsevier, Chapter 18. https://www.povertyactionlab.org/sites/default/files/documents/handbook_Rothstein_vonWachter_20160706.pdf (accessed May 23, 2017).

Thaler, Richard H., and Cass R. Sunstein. 2009. *Nudge: Improving Decisions about Health, Wealth, and Happiness.* New York: Penguin Books.

U.S. Department of Labor (USDOL). 2012. "Mandatory Disclosure of Unemployment Compensation Information for Department of Labor Evaluations of Unemployment Compensation Programs." Unemployment Insurance Program Letter No. 23-12. Washington, DC: U.S. Department of Labor.

Wandner, Stephen A. 2010. *Solving the Reemployment Puzzle: From Research to Policy.* Kalamazoo, MI: W.E. Upjohn Institute for Employment Research.

Chapter 2

How On-the-Ground Realities Shape the Design, Implementation, and Results of Experimental Studies

Irma Perez-Johnson
Annalisa Mastri
Samia Amin
Mathematica Policy Research

Planning and implementing a large-scale experimental evaluation of a social program is not unlike planning and embarking on a major road trip. Before leaving, we carefully plot the route, identify likely stopping points, book needed accommodations, and even check for road construction and other potential obstacles along the way. Similarly, a significant amount of effort is invested up front in the design and planning for the launch of an experimental study. One specifies the intervention's theory of change or logic model, identifies the outcomes of interest, determines necessary sample sizes, specifies random-assignment procedures, identifies the data sources and analytic methods that will be used to evaluate results, recruits study sites, and generally tries to plan for all the needed details and anticipate as many roadblocks as possible.

Despite all this planning, the one certainty in both major road trips and experimental studies is that one will encounter unanticipated challenges and will have to adapt quickly. Evaluators need to balance the ideal with the practical while maintaining analytical rigor. For instance, when conducting a study of a program being implemented in multiple sites, often the ideal would be for all study sites to offer identical services to clients, delivered by staff with similar backgrounds and training, and with the same level of resources. But this is rarely feasible.

This chapter draws on our experiences designing and implementing three experimental studies of social programs to discuss how "on the ground" realities can shape the design, implementation, and results of such studies. We first provide some background on each study, then discuss considerations for designing, executing, and interpreting the results of such studies. We conclude with a summary of lessons that can inform similar efforts moving forward.

THREE ILLUSTRATIVE EXPERIMENTAL STUDIES

We draw on our experiences from three large-scale experimental studies sponsored by the U.S. Department of Labor (USDOL): 1) the Individual Training Account Experiment (ITA Experiment), 2) the Workforce Investment Act Adult and Dislocated Worker Programs Gold Standard Evaluation (WIA Evaluation), and 3) the Self-Employment Training Demonstration (SET Demonstration). The ITA Experiment and the WIA Evaluation were conducted within the context of ongoing programs under the Workforce Investment Act of 1998 (WIA). The SET Demonstration project was designed to show proof-of-concept—that is, to test whether a new program could be implemented with fidelity to the model and achieve the desired effects. Although all three studies took place in workforce-related settings with individual job seekers, many of the lessons learned from these experiments can be applied more broadly to experimental studies of human services programs.

The Individual Training Account Experiment

The ITA Experiment examined the effectiveness of three alternative models of delivering WIA-funded training vouchers, known as ITAs. Although WIA directed states to restrict available training programs for local high-demand occupations, it also gave states considerable flexibility in structuring their ITAs. For example, states could vary the amount of money they offered to trainees, the counseling supports offered, and the amount of counseling they required trainees to complete before getting access to an ITA (Perez-Johnson et al. 2000). The ITA Experiment sought to determine the optimal combinations of training dollars and counseling supports by testing the following three approaches:

1) **Guided choice.** This option featured fixed-amount and moderately sized ITAs ($3,500 on average) and some mandatory counseling activities to guide trainees' program choices. Guided choice was designed to resemble the widespread practice used in the early 2000s, when the study was launched (Trutko and Barnow 1999).

2) **Structured choice.** In this option, trainees could receive customized ITAs with a higher cap (around $7,500) but were required to complete more intensive counseling, and caseworkers could veto training choices on which they expected to have low labor-market returns.

3) **Maximum choice.** In this option, customers received the same ITA amount as under guided choice. Counseling to discuss training options, although available, was not required. Trainees had to request counseling if they wanted it.

The experiment took place in eight Local Workforce Investment Areas (LWIAs) across the United States. A total of 7,920 participants were randomly assigned to one of the three ITA approaches (Perez-Johnson et al. 2004). Staff in each LWIA worked with customers in all three study groups to avoid staff-specific effects on participants' outcomes, and all participants in each study site had the same menu of training programs to choose from. The experiment compared participants' training and earnings outcomes for up to seven years after entry into the study (Perez-Johnson, Moore, and Santillano 2011).

The WIA Adult and Dislocated Worker Programs Gold Standard Evaluation

The WIA Evaluation (Mastri et al. 2015) aimed to estimate the relative effectiveness of three tiers of services offered through the WIA Adult and Dislocated Worker Programs:

1) **Core services.** Available to all customers, core services typically include self-service activities such as accessing job listings and local labor market information in a resource room or on the Internet.

2) **Core and intensive services.** Customers who are unable to get a job that would lead to self-sufficiency using core services alone may access intensive services. These services can include customers working with a counselor to develop an employment plan and obtain in-depth assessments of their skills, interests, and abilities.

3) **The full WIA offering (core + intensive + training).** Customers who need a skills upgrade to obtain or retain employment can request ITAs to fund training from approved providers.

The WIA Evaluation was designed to produce nationally representative impacts. Therefore, the study first randomly selected LWIAs nationwide and then convinced them to participate in the study. In these LWIAs, almost all customers who requested and were eligible for WIA intensive services or training and who consented to participate in the study were randomly assigned to one of the three groups described above. Study intake occurred between November 2011 and February 2013, with intake durations varying between 2 and 16 months across the participating LWIAs. Across the 28 LWIAs that participated in the study, 35,665 customers were randomly assigned to one of the three groups. The evaluation examined the service receipt and labor market outcomes of study participants measured at 15 months and 30 months after their enrollment in the study.

The Self-Employment Training Demonstration

The ongoing SET Demonstration is testing strategies to support dislocated workers who want to start their own businesses (Amin et al. 2016). Unemployed and underemployed workers who propose establishing businesses in their fields of expertise are eligible for the program. Eligible applicants are randomly assigned either to a treatment group that gets access to SET services, in addition to whatever other services are available in the local area, or to a control group, which cannot access the SET program but can seek out the other services available in the area. The treatment group participants can receive up to 12 months of counseling, training, and technical assistance on business development from experienced providers, as well as up to $1,000 in seed capital microgrants to help them establish their businesses. As noted, the SET Demonstration was designed to illustrate proof-of-concept of a new program rather than evaluate existing services. Thus, the SET program itself had to first be developed alongside the evaluation, then sites selected to implement it. The program is being tested in four metropolitan areas across the United States (Chicago; Cleveland; Los Angeles; and Portland, Oregon). Enrollment occurred between July 2013 and February 2016, yielding a sample of 1,981 study participants. The evaluation will use survey data to measure SET's impact on receipt of self-employment assistance services, self-employment experiences, employment and earnings (both from self-employment and from wage/salary jobs), and job satisfaction. It is also drawing on qualitative data from site visits, phone interviews, and a management information system to examine program implementation.

HOW ON-THE-GROUND REALITIES SHAPE THE DESIGN, IMPLEMENTATION, AND RESULTS OF EXPERIMENTAL STUDIES

With the key features of these studies in mind, we now discuss how real-world factors frequently affect the design, implementation, and interpretation of results of experimental studies. The design phase encompasses everything from specifying the research questions of interest to conducting power calculations and identifying and recruiting sites that are suitable for the evaluation. The implementation phase includes a period of training for participating sites in study procedures, the study intake period, and the period of data collection and analysis. The results phase focuses on interpreting the study's results in light of the design and implementation experiences. Finally, we discuss special considerations for demonstration programs such as SET.

Study Design

The first phase in which on-the-ground realities begin to shape the experimental study is during the study's design phase. Key considerations include the following:

Selecting policy-relevant treatment contrasts

The study will have the most potential to detect program impacts if it can compare program receipt with the absence of similar services (i.e., a no-treatment control condition) or compare treatments that differ notably along key dimensions (i.e., contrasting important alternative approaches). A no-treatment counterfactual may be infeasible for an experimental study in the case of mandated or entitlement programs that do not allow denial of services to eligible individuals. In these cases, an experimental design could involve randomly assigning additional program components on top of entitled services, but it could not deny entitled services to form a control group. For instance,

WIA mandates universal access to core services. Therefore, the WIA Evaluation had to be designed so that all study participants could receive core services, and the study randomly assigned those who could receive intensive counseling and training services on top of core services. This made it impossible for the study to determine the overall effectiveness of WIA relative to no access to any WIA service.

Depending on the study's goals, comparing alternative approaches may be the preferred design even if a no-treatment contrast is feasible. For instance, in the ITA Experiment, the goal was to determine the optimal approach to structure ITAs, rather than to assess the net impacts of ITA training. In that case, it did not make sense to have a control group with no access to ITAs. For the WIA Experiment, the treatment-control contrasts would have been greater if study participants didn't have access to Wagner-Peyser Act employment services, which in some LWIAs are very similar to intensive services. But restricting study participants' access to Wagner-Peyser services would have represented a counterfactual that does not exist in reality, making the study's results less policy relevant. Similarly, in the SET study, the objective was to learn whether having the opportunity to participate in SET would result in better outcomes than having access to the usual infrastructure for business development support. In this scenario, it did not make sense, nor was it feasible, to ask partner providers or others to refuse their usual services to members of the SET control group.

Researchers and the policymakers interested in the studies' results must recognize in advance the potential limitations of the study findings. For example, in the ITA Experiment, a finding of no differences between the study groups would not imply that training was ineffective, just that the various voucher approaches did not change customer outcomes. Similarly, the SET study can show whether *enhanced* self-employment services matter, but not whether self-employment services in general are effective. Null findings from alternative treatment contrasts must be interpreted carefully, and a no-service control group can typically answer a broader set of policy-relevant questions.

Matching data collection plans with desired indicators

Ideally, the outcomes of interest to the study align well with the anticipated effects of the intervention being tested and are already captured in administrative data sources. However, these conditions frequently do not hold. For instance, in the SET Demonstration, the intervention was expected to affect self-employment activities and success rates of new businesses started by study participants. But data on these key outcomes of interest are not currently contained in administrative databases. Self-employment activities are not reportable to the state unemployment insurance reporting system, which is the typical source of administrative data on people's earnings. Thus, the study team decided early on that a survey of study participants would be necessary to collect key outcomes.

Collecting information on the treatment group's service receipt is important for interpreting the study's results. However, programs' management information systems do not always collect service receipt data at the level of detail ideal for the study. Moreover, it is rarely the case that these systems collect data on services that treatment-group members receive outside the program or on any services that control-group members receive. In addition, program staff often differ in the extent to which they update administrative systems with such information. For the SET Demonstration, participants' service receipt and achievement of program milestones were critical components of illustrating proof-of-concept. Therefore, the study team offered service providers financial incentives to record information on participants' progress through SET in a study-designed tracking system.

Finally, collecting information on control group members' service receipt is often important in understanding the counterfactual condition and interpreting the study's results. This is especially true in service-rich environments, where control-group members might be receiving services that are very similar to those of treatment-group members. This was the case in the SET study, and surveys are usually the best source of these data.

To be sure, there are some instances where the context in which the program operates facilitates use of existing data sources. For instance, a program implemented in a workforce system setting among a segment of job-seeking customers might be able to use administrative data the workforce system is already collecting on all customers to examine the employment outcomes of participants. Care must be taken in the design phase, however, to assess not only the feasibility of using existing administrative data sources but also the quality of these data, and to develop a backup plan if appropriate.

Short-listing good candidates for the study

Not all sites are good candidates for inclusion in an experimental study. Some are in the midst of making big changes to their programming or organizational structures. Others may be reluctant to participate in an experimental study, or are already participating in a different study. And some sites will simply lack the client flow necessary for participating in a study.

For the WIA Evaluation, we began with a list of the full set of LWIAs nationwide. Given the evaluation's target sample sizes and intake period, we excluded LWIAs serving fewer than 100 customers per year. Not having adequate client flow can be even more of an issue for experimental studies of grant programs that might only award enough funds to serve a relatively small number of customers in each site, meaning that many sites would need to participate in the study in order to detect meaningful impacts. In some cases, there simply might not be enough total participants over the study's time frame to support an experimental study.

Recruiting enough suitable sites to participate in the study

Having an adequate number of sites participating in the study is critical for being able to detect meaningful program impacts. However, recruiting sites is rarely a straightforward process, even when there are a number of potentially suitable sites for the evaluation. For the ITA Experiment, USDOL issued a request for proposals to interested LWIAs or consortia of agencies, and only six expressed interest in implementing the experiment, despite generous financial incentives to do so. For the SET Demonstration, the study team preselected six metropolitan areas in six states that met the necessary conditions for the study and conducted targeted outreach to them. LWIAs in one metropolitan area were keen to participate but did not have sufficient provider capacity to implement the model as planned. LWIAs in another metropolitan area did not want to participate because of concerns about staff burden.

The WIA Evaluation faced an additional challenge. To be nationally representative, the study needed to first randomly select LWIAs nationwide and then convince them to participate in the study. We aimed to include 30 LWIAs in the study and successfully recruited 26 (87 percent) of these. In addition, we recruited two others that were randomly selected to replace two of the four local areas that declined to participate, for a total of 28 local areas participating in the study.

For all three studies, our recruitment efforts succeeded because we did the following:

We involved all key stakeholders in recruitment presentations and meetings. Having all interested parties at the table is important for achieving buy-in. For the WIA Evaluation, we first had to identify who the relevant stakeholders were in each LWIA. In some, the LWIA could not agree to participate without support from the state, so state representatives were involved. Some potential sites asked us to present in front of their local boards. Others asked us to meet with line staff or staff from partner organizations or referral sources. For SET, we conducted a series of recruitment e-mails and calls—first with regional and state officials from both the UI office and the workforce development departments. We followed up these initial contacts with meetings with the local workforce agencies. We wrapped up with in-person visits to each of the promising sites.

We demonstrated that we had the strong commitment and support of USDOL. For the WIA evaluation, federal USDOL staff participated in recruiting trips, the assistant secretary of labor sent letters to LWIAs and also made phone calls to some of the more reluctant sites, and USDOL staff held a special session at a conference attended by LWIA representatives to discuss the importance of the study. For SET, senior USDOL staff wrote e-mails to invite participation and participated in site recruitment calls.

We offered compensation. The WIA, ITA, and SET studies all provided sites with payments to offset the staff time associated with implementing study procedures and cooperating with evaluation activities. These payments could be used, for example, to hire an additional staff person to assist with data entry or documentation needed for the study (e.g., assembling and securely storing study forms), or to hire an additional staff person to handle the added caseload.

We offered concessions to make the experiment more attractive to sites. The design phase is a good time to start thinking through parts of the experiment that might be contentious from the standpoint of the sites. Even when sites are mandated to participate in an experiment (for instance, as a condition of receiving grant funding), researchers want to ensure their buy-in for the study so that they maximize the study's potential success. Common sticking points include the following three:

1) **Denying services to customers in the control group(s).** Program staff are motivated by a desire to help their customers and often find the idea of denying services unpalatable. They also might be reluctant to deny services because it could result in unused capacity at their programs. A potential solution to both problems is to reduce the ratio of participants that are denied services. Although having equally sized treatment and control groups is optimal from a statistical power standpoint, sites may be more comfort-

able with randomization if a smaller proportion of participants are turned away. For the WIA Evaluation, we determined the total sample size needs with an average random-assignment rate of around 6 percent each to the core and core-and-intensive groups. The other 88 percent of customers were randomly assigned to the group that could receive full WIA services as usual. However, these study group assignment rates were possible because of the large study sample size.

2) **Implementing burdensome study procedures.** If sites perceive that they will have to engage in burdensome documentation or other study procedures, they will be less likely to cooperate. During the design phase, steps can be taken to reduce the study's burden on participating sites. For instance, for the SET Demonstration, we developed an online orientation video and online participant application to save American Job Center staff from conducting these in person. The study team also planned to review applications, make eligibility determinations, conduct random assignment, and refer individuals accepted into SET to the local microenterprise providers who provided services. For the WIA Evaluation, staff at American Job Centers had to conduct the random assignment, so we developed an easy-to-use online random-assignment system that would only require staff to enter minimal information as data.

3) **Concern about the effects on the program's performance.** Program administrators may worry about how the study will affect the extent to which they meet or exceed legislatively mandated performance targets. Depending on the study design, this could occur because the programs will be serving fewer total customers (since some will be assigned to the control group) or because some of the particularly promising customers—who would have contributed favorably to the program's performance reporting—will be

assigned to the control group and hence not be included in the reporting. In the case of demonstration programs, desired outcomes for the new project might not align with the existing performance measures. Efforts can be made to see whether program offices can relax or adapt performance requirements for the duration of the study.

Implementing the Study

Often, we can anticipate during the design phase many of the challenges of implementing a social experiment in the context that we are studying, and we begin adapting the study design at that point. But ultimately the success of the evaluation hinges on how well the evaluation team adapts and responds to challenges encountered during the evaluation's implementation. Key challenges we frequently have faced and to which we have had to adapt include the following:

Achieving buy-in of program staff

Even after sites have agreed to participate in a study—a decision that is often made at the administrative or higher level—frontline staff working directly with participants might still not understand the value of an experimental study. It is particularly of concern when the control group will not have access to study services and cannot find alternative services in the community. Sometimes program staff have such dedication to serving their clients that they are resistant to participating in the study or following study procedures.

Explaining the importance of the study in easy-to-understand terms is critical to achieving staff buy-in. For the WIA Evaluation, we developed a presentation and accompanying one-page fact sheet aimed at line staff and supervisors. We delivered the presentation during site recruitment visits and distributed the fact sheets throughout the course of the evaluation. Both described the study's importance, goals, and basic outlines of the design in layman's terms. In particular, they centered on why random assignment is the strongest research design, why it is ethical, and how the study's results would be used to make future funding decisions, allowing program staff to continue or even expand their good work.

Building capacity of program staff to implement study procedures correctly

Program staff are typically not accustomed to explaining a research study to potential participants, obtaining their consent to participate, entering information into a tracking or random-assignment system, conducting random assignment, and informing study participants of their study-group assignments. Yet successfully implementing each of these steps is critical to the success of the experimental study.

To address these challenges for the WIA Evaluation, the study team thoroughly investigated the program service delivery structure, customer flow, and staffing, and developed study procedures customized for each site in order to be as seamless as possible with existing service delivery. The study team developed customized study procedure manuals documenting in detail each step that program staff had to take for the study. The manuals included explanations of the study forms, scripts for explaining the study to customers and collecting their consent, and detailed information on how to use the random-assignment system. Information was presented in multiple ways—for instance, as scripts and as talking points that staff could adapt to their own style. We conducted a day-long training at each site for staff to go over the study procedures in detail and to allow staff the opportunity to practice role playing. Early training sessions revealed that, in our zealousness to provide sites with lots of details and many options for conveying information to study participants, some staff felt overwhelmed by the volume of information provided. So we developed a reference guide that boiled down the study procedures manual into a 10-page document that staff could more easily reference on a daily basis.

The SET Demonstration took a different approach. The study team limited LWIA responsibilities to referring potential clients to the SET website so they didn't have to deal with complex study procedures. As described above, the study team handled orientations, applications, random assignment, and client referral to services. Nonetheless, since only one out of our four sites was familiar with self-employment services, we still had to build LWIA capacity for promoting this new kind of program. To do so, we provided detailed procedure manuals, in-person training, scripts for describing the SET program, and attractive brochures and fliers to help promote SET.

We learned over time, however, that just simplifying the procedures and initial training was not sufficient. One unintended side effect of not involving LWIA staff in orientations and intake for SET was that they were less familiar with the program and less invested in its success. Capacity building therefore became an ongoing effort. We discuss below how we created feedback loops to address this issue.

Reserving resources to maintain buy-in and capacity for the evaluation

Commitment, energy, and attention to the evaluation may wane over the course of implementation. Initially, sites may be excited about what they can learn through participation, or—in the case of demonstration projects—about the prospect of offering new services to their customers. However, it takes enduring commitment on the part of program administrators and staff to follow through on that initial excitement. This is especially true in times when site partners are under strain—when resources run low, staff turnover is high, or staff face many competing responsibilities. In those circumstances, it can be asking a lot for sites and their staff to maintain their commitment and attention to a temporary initiative. It can be especially challenging in the case of demonstration projects in which a whole new program must be tested (see Box 2.1).

Supporting program staff to correctly implement study procedures cannot end with training. Study teams must devote resources to providing ample support throughout the study enrollment period and extra technical assistance when support and effort appear to be wan-

**Box 2.1   Special Considerations for Demonstration Projects:
Ensuring Program Fidelity**

The goal of a demonstration project is twofold: first, to provide "proof of concept" (i.e., a demonstration that a program can be successfully implemented while being faithful to the model) and, second, to evaluate the impacts of the program. Project staff must be prepared for the reality that *it can take time to implement the demonstration program with fidelity*. Program staff often struggle to deliver a new set of services as planned, especially when they are quite different from what they are used to delivering. This can result in delays in beginning to offer services in the first place, and in weak program implementation.

In some cases, monitoring to identify implementation difficulties and providing ongoing support to the sites can rectify these issues. For instance, early in the SET Demonstration, the study team noticed through visits to the SET service providers that case management services—a critical element of the program—were not being delivered as frequently or thoroughly as intended. The study team provided technical assistance on the case management model to 5 of the 11 service providers over three to eight months. The study team also initiated monthly phone calls to monitor implementation fidelity and provide an opportunity for SET service providers to ask questions of the evaluation team.

In other cases, the demonstration (or some aspect of it) proves difficult to implement because it is too much of a departure from standard practice. For instance, the Structured Choice approach in the ITA Experiment was not fully implemented because counselors felt uncomfortable vetoing customers' training choices. The study authors concluded that a substantial cultural shift would need to take place for program staff to successfully implement the Structured Choice approach (as originally envisioned) to administering ITAs. Notably, despite the more limited implementation of the Structured Choice approach in the ITA Experiment, it proved the most effective of the three ITA approaches tested (Perez-Johnson, Moore, and Santillano 2011).

ing. Training must be followed by monitoring phone calls with program staff and, if possible, site visits to understand the implementation challenges and determine how best to address them. These issues could range from the relatively insignificant, such as assembling forms in the wrong order, to the significant, such as not randomly assigning everyone who is eligible for the study. Designating a person from the evaluation team to serve as a liaison with each site can be an effective way to monitor implementation and handle questions or concerns from program staff; all three of our studies provided this. In addition, both the WIA Evaluation and the SET Demonstration operated hotlines for staff to call with questions.

For the SET Demonstration, the study team realized that, because SET was a new and temporary program (available for less than three years) and not directly provided by LWIA staff, workforce staff were promoting it less and less over time than they had at the beginning of operations. Moreover, budget pressures in the participating LWIAs were making it difficult for overburdened workforce and UI staff to focus on SET. The team introduced feedback loops to get the buy-in of the referral sources in the LWIAs. We sent monthly e-mail updates to all LWIAs on the progress of their recruitment efforts relative to other sites. This encouraged sites that were recruiting well to keep up the good work and motivated some of our lagging sites to become more competitive. For sites where recruitment was lagging, we conducted in-person visits to retrain and motivate staff and followed that up with biweekly calls. Sharing client success stories and testimonials proved to be a particularly effective strategy but was only feasible once the program had been in operation for a while. It helped to generate excitement about SET and made staff more comfortable in referring clients to the new program.

Increasing assistance when staff burden exceeds expectations

Except in rare cases, some interruptions to the ideal flow of services that staff provide and participants receive should be expected. Staff members, in addition to their regular duties, must perform study procedures and, in many cases, some data entry in support of the study. During the study implementation phase, they might find that implementing study procedures is taking longer than the evaluation team had anticipated, imposing unexpected burdens on program staff and causing errors in following study procedures.

One way to address any unanticipated burden is to offer additional compensation or other resources to local partners. For the SET Demonstration, for example, we provided additional funds to support special outreach activities such as mailings in sites where meeting recruiting targets required additional effort. For all of our sites, we provided additional supplies of publicity materials (fliers, brochures) whenever they were needed because these were expensive for our partner sites to produce. We also provided ongoing support by designating evaluation liaisons to each study site to help troubleshoot emerging challenges.

Developing new tools to minimize the burden on staff can also help. During the WIA Evaluation, some sites noted that introducing and explaining the evaluation was taking them substantially longer than anticipated. As a result, the evaluation team developed a video—much like the one used in the SET Demonstration—that staff could play for customers either at their desks or in a group orientation setting. This freed up staff to work on other tasks while the video played.

Another example was adding study group assignment to existing program management information systems. Because program staff conducted random assignment for the study, they had to enter some information about customers into an online random-assignment system we had designed for the study, and customers' study group assignments were recorded there. Although we had designed the system so that minimal data entry was required, some staff complained that they had to look up every customer with whom they met in the online system to see whether they were already enrolled in the evaluation and, if so, what services they were allowed to receive. They noted that it would be easier to look up this information in their existing management information systems, which they would be accessing anyway when working with customers. As a result, the evaluation team worked with data systems personnel at the state level to add fields with which to document study groups within the existing statewide management information system.

Documenting variations in service delivery across participating sites

Differences in staff backgrounds and training, program context, participant characteristics, and the way service providers are accustomed to delivering services mean that services that are nominally the same may not actually be delivered in exactly the same way across sites. For instance, WIA gives local areas considerable discretion in service delivery. We found that during the WIA Evaluation a core "job search workshop" varied in length from a couple of hours at one site to three days at another. It also was categorized as an intensive service at some sites but a core service at others.

In the ITA Experiment, the goal was for participating sites to implement the same three ITA approaches. However, ITA caps had varied across sites before the study, and sites needed to set the caps high enough that they would spend their entire training budget (or lose it the next year). As a result, the caps for each treatment arm necessarily varied across sites. Other variations included which occupations were considered high wage and high demand, whether assessments were required and used as a counseling tool, and supervisor involvement in the approval of customer training selections under the Structured Choice approach.

The SET Demonstration was designed to provide a common service flow across microenterprise service delivery providers, including individualized service planning, monthly check-ins, quarterly reassessments and service plan updates, and the $1,000 seed capital microgrant available to participants who met required milestones. Within these parameters, however, sites varied in how they structured their check-ins, the degree to which they relied on workshops and group classes, and the range of technical assistance and additional services they offered to SET participants. The infrastructure for self-employment support—e.g., the number or reach of individual providers and the overall culture of entrepreneurship—also varied across sites.

Documenting these variations is important for interpreting the findings of the impact analysis and providing lessons learned for program improvement. Large experimental evaluations often have an implementation study tied to them—particularly in the case of demonstration projects—in which qualitative researchers systematically collect information on many aspects of program organization, operations, and staffing, among other topics. This can be a rich source of information on variation in program delivery across participating study sites. Lower-cost methods such as phone calls with sites and online staff surveys can also be good sources of this information.

Addressing changes in service delivery in response to the study

Studies of ongoing programs would ideally examine the effectiveness of services as they are typically delivered. However, sometimes a service offering or its delivery changes in unexpected ways as a result of the study. In the ITA Experiment, some private training vendors appeared to change the content and price of their offerings in response to the study, bundling additional certificates together and charging a higher price because the ITA cap was higher for some customers as a result of the experiment. During the WIA Evaluation, staff in some local areas reported that referral sources such as local community colleges were "drying up" because of a misperception that the local area was no longer funding ITAs. And in evaluations where study enrollment is lower than anticipated, assigning a fraction of study participants to a control group may leave some slots unfilled. As a result, staff may find that they have more resources to serve any given customer, thereby allowing them to deliver more intensive services than they would in the absence of the study.

The study team must pay attention to these issues for the duration of the study enrollment and follow-up period and address any substantial changes in service delivery to the extent possible. Failure to do so could have significant implications, particularly if the program is so changed that it no longer provides an accurate picture of how the program will operate once the study is over. In other words, the evaluation is of a program that does not exist. In the case of the ITA Experiment, little could be done to change service provider prices or restrict participants from asking for ITA funds up to the cap available to them. For the WIA Evaluation, the study team worked with managers and administrators at the LWIA to coordinate outreach to their referral sources to explain the study and emphasize that training funds were still available.

Monitoring sample sizes and adjusting procedures accordingly

Recruitment often lags behind what was anticipated based on previous history or projected customer flow. If sample sizes substantially lag behind projections, the study will be less able to detect meaningful program impacts. Based on historical data on the number of customers served in participating LWIAs, the WIA Evaluation expected to enroll about 85,000 customers in the study. In actuality, only about 36,000 were enrolled. In the SET Demonstration, enrollment lagged substantially below targets, partly because the eligibility requirements were fairly narrow and partly because the high unemployment levels that prompted the demonstration in the first place had abated by the time the program began. In the ITA Experiment, the opposite happened—the economic downturn that occurred around the time of the study, which was unanticipated, increased the overall flow of customers and trainees through the participating LWIAs, resulting in much larger sample sizes over the study's two-year implementation period.

It is imperative that researchers monitor sample buildup and work with sites to understand and rectify, to the extent possible, problems with recruiting enough participants. The SET Demonstration revised outreach materials to make them simpler and more accessible to potential participants. They worked on achieving buy-in from LWIA staff so that they would spread the word and promote the demonstration program. They also tailored outreach tactics for each site, including boosting advertising efforts in some sites and even hiring a marketing firm for outreach in one site.

The WIA Evaluation encouraged program staff to tap their referral sources, but the main approach to combating lower-than-expected sample sizes was to adjust the rates at which customers in lagging sites were randomly assigned to the core or core-and-intensive groups. (As mentioned earlier, originally only 12 percent of all WIA customers were supposed to be referred to these two groups.) In short, achieving the target number of customers in these groups was crucial to maintaining the study's power. Since the total number of customers was lower than expected in some sites, we had to increase the proportion of customers assigned to these groups. In addition, the study enrollment period for some of the participating local areas was extended beyond the originally planned 12 months to allow for additional sample buildup. In the end, the study met its enrollment targets for customers assigned to the core and core-and-intensive groups.

Interpreting the Study's Results

The flexibility and adaptations the study team makes in response to the realities of designing and executing an experimental study in the context of social programs have implications for the interpretation of the study's results. Key challenges include the following:

The counterfactual is weaker than anticipated in some sites

The services available to control group members in the broader community often vary across sites, sometimes substantially. If control group members in sites with many similar alternative services make use of those services, the differences between the treatment and control groups are narrowed. This makes it more difficult for the study to detect impacts of the program. For example, in some LWIAs participating in the WIA Evaluation, there was no other public source of training funds available, whereas in others, alternative sources of training funds were readily available. This meant that the treatment-control contrast was weaker in the latter sites, again making it harder to detect program impacts.

If the suitability assessment conducted during the design phase identifies sites where a lot of alternative services are available, the study team can consider excluding such service-rich sites. Sometimes, however, the extent of alternatives available is not known until after the study is launched and data are collected. In those instances, the evaluation's results must be interpreted through the lens of what was actually being tested on the ground, and not in theory. Doing this requires investigating and documenting the services available to the control group and, if possible, capturing control-group service receipt. When statistical power allows, impacts can be investigated by site and compared among those with strong treatment-control differentials and those with weaker ones.

The sample size is lower than anticipated

Strategies to increase recruitment and enrollment in programs are not always effective, and sample sizes can fall short of targets. There are limited options available in this scenario. If the analysis was planned to be done by site, the data analysis could instead pool the sites to boost statistical power. However, the conceptual model of the program and the research questions of interest would have to suggest that pooling could be appropriate. For instance, it might not make sense to pool sites with completely different service delivery strategies and target populations, even if they are funded by the same grant.

In these scenarios, conducting post hoc power analyses is useful for determining the magnitude of effects the study can detect, given its realized sample sizes. This can help policymakers and others better interpret the study's findings. For instance, a large but statistically insignificant point estimate could indicate a lack of statistical power, rather than the lack of a true impact of the program on the outcome of interest.

Sample attrition is high

Sometimes it can be difficult to locate study participants for follow-up data collection efforts. This is especially true when the program under study targets a hard-to-reach population, such as homeless people or formerly incarcerated adults. When experiments have high overall study attrition, or large differences in attrition rates between the treatment and control groups, the amount of bias in the impact estimates rises, making us less confident in the study's results. The What Works Clearinghouse, a systematic evidence review project funded by the U.S. Department of Education, developed a bias model that specifies the combinations of overall and differential attrition that are acceptable in experimental studies. Studies that exceed the specified thresholds are considered to have a high likelihood of biased impact estimates.

In cases of high overall or differential sample attrition, a carefully controlled analysis is one approach to reducing bias in the estimated impacts. Ideally, the authors would include controls for the demographic characteristics of the study sample and preprogram measures of the outcomes that are of interest to the study. In a study examining the impact of a job training program on earnings, this preprogram measure could include the earnings history of participants leading up to the point of random assignment.[1] Another approach is to explicitly demonstrate that the study participants included in the analysis sample (i.e., those for whom follow-up data were available) were similar in preprogram demographics and outcomes at the time of random assignment. This can be done by performing statistical tests of the baseline differences between the study groups. However, ultimately, high attrition of study participants cannot be "controlled away," and many evidence reviews would downgrade such studies.

LESSONS LEARNED

In this paper, we've sought to draw on experiences in designing and conducting three large-scale experimental studies to discuss how on-the-ground realities influence the design, implementation, and results of these studies. In many cases, a flexible and adaptable approach to the evaluation can mitigate the issues encountered. We hope that the lessons we have learned from these and other evaluations can inform future efforts. Specifically, we offer the following advice:

- When selecting sites for the evaluation, think carefully about the objectives of the study and the characteristics of the sites that could potentially participate. Are they strong or weak implementers? Do they likely have sufficient sample size? What is the availability of similar services in the community? Balance the needs for representativeness and for evaluating the program as closely as possible to how it would operate in the absence of the study against the need for feasibility in successfully implementing the study at the site.

- When recruiting sites to participate in an experiment, prepare easy-to-understand materials about the goals and benefits of the study and its ethics. Have in mind concessions that could be offered to the sites to minimize the impact of study participation on their service delivery. Make sure all stakeholders are at the table during the recruiting process.

- If possible, involve federal sponsors of the study during site recruitment and throughout the course of the evaluation to demonstrate a commitment to and support of the study.

- For demonstrations, recruit sites with a strong commitment to and interest in the concept being tested, as well as interest in learning from the study's results. Build feedback loops for staff and program administrators to learn how the demonstration program operates in practice, what services are provided to referred clients, and what benefits participants derive from the opportunity to participate. This information is critical to sustain enthusiasm for the program and a commitment to offering the program to suitable candidates.

- If study resources permit, compensate sites for their time and effort spent implementing the study—this helps to achieve buy-in, facilitates site recruitment, and lessens the burden on site staff.

- Develop both detailed manuals and easy-to-use resources to support implementation; quick reference guides are key. For demonstrations, be clear on the elements that must be preserved and those that can be adapted; aim for flexibility wherever possible.

- Reserve resources to provide lots of training and ongoing support for the study sites. Designate a site liaison to facilitate communication about the evaluation, monitor site progress early to correct any mistakes, and monitor sites on an ongoing basis to ensure they maintain their focus on and fidelity to evaluation procedures. Adapt the frequency and intensity of monitoring as needed. Implementation issues can evolve and change over time, especially in the context of a multiyear program. For instance, staff turnover, the business cycle, and spikes or severe dips in application rates or program referrals can all affect study implementation at various points in time.

- Take proactive steps to minimize the burden on local staff. For example, automate procedures to the extent possible and, if feasible, embed data collection into existing management information systems. Provide ready-made resources for staff, such as promotional brochures and posters, run help lines to handle questions about the program, and designate a single point of contact from the study team to handle questions or concerns from local staff. Share information about burden-reducing and other facilitating strategies or resources that participating sites develop on their own.

•

- Document variation in program implementation and services available to the control group to help interpret results.

- If, despite the adaptations made along the way, issues remain with the implementation of the experiment, conduct supplementary analyses when possible and discuss the results. For instance, conduct post hoc power analyses if sample sizes are low, change the analysis approach if implementation was not strong in some sites or the treatment-control contrast was weak, and include controls or demonstrate baseline equivalence if attrition was high. Although these methods might not answer the original research questions of interest with the level of rigor originally intended, they can still provide meaningful answers to important questions about the effectiveness of programs under study.

Note

The projects discussed in this chapter were funded, either wholly or in part, with federal funds from the U.S. Department of Labor, Employment and Training Administration. The contents of this chapter do not necessarily reflect the views or policies of USDOL, nor does mention of trade names, commercial products, or organizations imply endorsement of same by the U.S. government.

1. Some systematic evidence reviews, including the Clearinghouse for Labor Evaluation and Research, require that earnings and employment history be measured for more than one year before random assignment to guard against the Ashenfelter dip.

References

Amin, Samia, Heinrich Hock, Irma Perez-Johnson, Shawn Marsh, Mary Anne Anderson, and Rob Fairlie. 2016. *Evaluation of the Self-Employment Training Demonstration: Design Report.* Princeton, NJ: Mathematica Policy Research.

Mastri, Annalisa, Sheena McConnell, Linda Rosenberg, Peter Schochet, Dana Rotz, Andrew Clarkwest, Ken Fortson, AnnaMaria McCutcheon, Katie Bodenlos, Jessica Ziegler, and Paul Burkander. 2015. *Evaluating National Ongoing Programs: Implementing the WIA Adult and Dislocated Worker Programs Gold Standard Evaluation.* Submitted to the U.S. Department of Labor, Employment and Training Administration. Washington, DC: Mathematica Policy Research.

Perez-Johnson, Irma, Paul Decker, Sheena McConnell, Robert Olsen, Jacquelyn Anderson, Ronald D'Amico, and Jeffrey Salzman. 2000. *The Individual Training Account Demonstration: Design Report.* Washington, DC: Mathematica Policy Research.

Perez-Johnson, Irma, Sheena McConnell, Paul T. Decker, Jeanne Bellotti, Jeffrey Salzman, and Jessica Pearlman. 2004. *The Effects of Customer Choice: First Findings from the Individual Training Account Experiment.* Princeton, NJ: Mathematica Policy Research.

Perez-Johnson, Irma, Quinn Moore, and Robert Santillano. 2011. *Improving the Effectiveness of Individual Training Accounts: Long-Term Findings from an Experimental Evaluation of Three Service Delivery Models.* Princeton, NJ: Mathematica Policy Research.

Trutko, John W., and Burt S. Barnow. 1999. "Experiences with Job Training Vouchers under the Job Training Partnership Act and Implications for Individual Training Accounts under the Workforce Investment Act." Unpublished paper. Washington, DC: U.S. Department of Labor, Employment and Training Administration.

Chapter 3

An Example of a Low-Cost Intervention to Target Services to Participants of a Local Welfare-to-Work Program

Randall W. Eberts
W.E. Upjohn Institute for Employment Research

This chapter shows how low-cost interventions can be integrated into the operations of existing workforce programs. Recent interest in using lessons from behavioral economics to improve participation and engagement in social programs has led to a growing number of initiatives. These initiatives have attempted to use randomized controlled trial (RCT) experiments to improve program design, particularly in the way information is presented to participants. The administration of President Obama made this approach a priority in how it administered social programs. In 2014 the administration created the Social and Behavioral Sciences Team (SBST), dubbed the "Nudge Squad"—presumably after Richard Thaler and Cass Sunstein's (2008) influential book titled *Nudge*. Their book documents the use of behavioral science in improving participation in social programs and thus the effectiveness of the programs. Even before the creation of the SBST, the administration used lessons from behavioral economics in designing certain programs included in the American Recovery and Reinvestment Act so that consumers would respond more quickly and effectively to the economic stimulus initiatives. This result will be elaborated upon in Chapter 5.

The United Kingdom (UK) has also pursued lessons from the insights of behavioral economics. In 2010 the UK Cabinet Office established the Behavioural Insights Team for the purpose of finding "intelligent ways to encourage, support and enable people to make better choices for themselves" (Behavioural Insights Team 2011, p. 3). One of its first interventions was to work with staff from Jobcentre Plus offices, which are similar to the U.S. One-Stop Career Centers, to redesign the process individuals go through when they sign on to receive benefits and begin their job search process. Since then, the Behavioural Insights Team has conducted more than 150 randomized controlled trials evaluating interventions in a wide variety of social areas.[1]

According to a survey paper by Babcock et al. (2012), "behavioral economics stresses empirical findings of behavior that are partially at odds with standard economic assumptions. The key empirical findings from field research in behavioral economics suggest that individuals can make systematic errors or be put off by complexity, that they procrastinate, and that they hold nonstandard preferences and nonstandard beliefs" (p. 2). Therefore, insights from behavioral economics focus on ways to simplify complex decision-making processes that may tax the ability of individuals to navigate government programs effectively. The SBST projects in the United States and the Behavioural Insights Team initiatives in Great Britain are designed primarily to address the behavioral barriers that affect how people engage with programs (National Science and Technology Council 2015). While the expected results may be modest, so are the costs, which could lead to large returns on investment.

The Obama administration formalized the use of behavioral insights by directing federal agencies to initiate and test such procedures. In 2013 the administration sent a memo to the heads of federal agencies stating that "many innovative companies use rapidly conducted randomized field trials to identify high impact innovations and move them quickly into production."[2] While randomized controlled trials are not a new approach to evaluating social programs, in the past, most RCT evaluations were hugely expensive and took years to conduct and analyze. The approach advocated by the Obama administration was to try to streamline the evaluation process by embedding the process within the programs receiving the interventions. This is possible if agencies already collect data that record participant outcomes and characteristics and if participants can easily be randomly selected into control groups and treatment groups.

For example, a conference on RCT held in the summer of 2014 and sponsored by the Office of Technology Policy and the Coalition for Evidence-Based Policy explored effective ways to embed low-cost RCTs in government social programs. Participants asserted that the following three steps should be taken: 1) acquire greater research access to government administrative data, such as unemployment insurance (UI) wage records for workforce programs, with appropriate privacy protections; 2) generate increased government funding opportunities that specifically focus on low-cost RCTs; and 3) create more high-profile competitions and challenges for low-cost RCTs, such as those launched by the Coalition for Evidence-Based Policy (Shankar 2014).

Missing from this list of necessary steps for carrying out low-cost RCTs, particularly for public workforce development programs, is the willingness of state and local agencies to participate in such programs. Directing federal agencies to pursue low-cost RCTs may be the first step, but in a decentralized workforce system—which is the approach taken in the United States in which state and local agencies have considerable autonomy in deciding whether they would like to participate in activities such as RCTs—it is necessary to consider the motivations and incentives for them to be involved. Without local involvement, it is impossible to embed behavioral insight–related interventions into most government social programs.

Despite the intense interest by the Obama administration in using low-cost RCTs to evaluate the effectiveness of behavioral insights in federal programs, few initiatives were directed at workforce programs.[3] The 2015 and 2016 annual reports of the SBST list nearly 40 projects, and only 2 involve federal workforce programs (National Science and Technology Council 2015, 2016). At least one effort to conduct a low-cost RCT at local workforce investment boards was thwarted by the boards' reluctance to participate. Consequently, it is paramount to identify local workforce boards with interested staff and an organizational and incentive structure conducive to undertaking these experiments.

Therefore, the purpose of this chapter is twofold. First, it describes the prerequisites for successful implementation of such interventions in workforce programs, including incentives to enlist local workforce boards. Second, it describes a program that successfully integrated a simple but effective low-cost intervention and evaluation into a workforce program. While the program described here is not new (the pilot was conducted in the late 1990s and early 2000s) and has been reported in previous publications, it still is instructive in providing an example that may guide the implementation of future initiatives.[4] Furthermore, since the program has already been evaluated using RCT, which was embedded in the intervention, the outcomes of the intervention are available, whereas many of the more recent projects are still awaiting the completion of an evaluation.

THE FEDERAL GOVERNMENT'S INTEREST IN LOW-COST RCTs

By establishing the Social and Behavioral Sciences Team in 2014, the Obama administration institutionalized the use of behavioral insights at the federal level. SBST was a cross-agency team, housed in the White House Office of Science and Technology Policy, with the purpose of translating findings and methods from the social and behavioral sciences into improvements in federal policies and programs (National Science and Technology Council 2015).[5] During its first year of operation, its team focused on executing proof-of-concept projects in which behavioral insights could be embedded directly into programs at a low cost and could lead to quantifiable and immediate improvements in program outcomes. The team pursued two areas where behavioral science could play a significant role: 1) improving access to programs and 2) improving government efficiency. Seventeen projects are listed in the SBST 2015 annual report; these include promoting retirement savings, improving college access, increasing medical insurance coverage, and reducing delinquent debt repayments, among several others. Many of the projects included simple ways to communicate with individuals to improve their engagement in federal programs.

On September 15, 2015, behavioral insights were further codified into federal social policy when President Obama signed an executive order that encouraged federal agencies to "design . . . policies and programs to reflect our best understanding of how people engage with, participate in, use, and respond to those policies and programs." In the words of the order, it specifically directed agencies to take the following four actions:

1)   Identify opportunities to help qualifying individuals, families, communities, and businesses access public programs and benefits by . . . removing administrative hurdles, shortening wait times, and simplifying forms;

2)   Improve how information is presented to consumers . . . by considering how the content, format, timing, and medium by which information is conveyed affects comprehension and action by individuals, as appropriate;

3)   Identify programs that offer choices and carefully consider how the presentation and structure of those choices, including the order, number, and arrangement of options, can most effectively promote public welfare, as appropriate, giving particular consideration to the selection and setting of default options; and

4)   Review elements of their policies and programs that are designed to encourage or make it easier for Americans to take specific actions . . . (White House 2015).

WILLINGNESS OF STATE AND LOCAL AGENCIES TO CONDUCT BEHAVIORAL EXPERIMENTS

While a presidential executive order, like the one President Obama issued incorporating behavioral insights into federal programs, gets the attention of federal officials, it may not be as effective in eliciting the participation of states and local agencies. The nation's workforce system, currently operating under the Workforce Innovation and Opportunity Act (WIOA), is a federal-state-local partnership. Most funding and guidelines originate from the federal government, but the local workforce investment boards (WIBs) have direct responsibility for delivering the services to customers. The WIBs develop strategic plans that target services to meet the needs of customers (both job seekers and employers) and contract with local providers to deliver services. While they must meet the requirements of WIOA, the local boards and their staff have some discretion in the operations, including whether to participate in additional programs or activities that may be beyond the scope of the WIOA legislation and state mandates.

The willingness of states and local workforce boards to participate in programs that involve low-cost RCTs, or even in large-scale evaluations funded by the U.S. Department of Labor, varies widely. Stephen Wandner, the editor of this volume and a longtime USDOL official involved with federal evaluations, describes in his book *Solving the Reemployment Puzzle* the negotiations required between USDOL and the states to implement various large-scale evaluation projects. He writes that establishing what became known as the New Jersey Experiment, one of the most consequential evaluations of workforce programs and UI systems, rested on convincing the state of New Jersey to participate. Issues included the following three: 1) providing funding for the state to cover additional costs, including alteration of regular services to accommodate the evaluation; 2) determining whether state officials would be willing to participate in a randomized controlled trial in which a preselected group of customers are denied services; and 3) addressing the concern of state officials as to whether the results would shine a favorable light on New Jersey. Ultimately, the state agreed to serve as the demonstration site and was awarded $4.7 million for operating the evaluation when the program began in 1986 (Wandner 2010).

Many of the same issues that confront a state in deciding to conduct a large evaluation, such as the New Jersey Experiment, also confront a local WIB in deciding whether to engage in a low-cost RCT. Are staff interested in exploring ways to improve the services they offer to customers? Can they come up with possible interventions on their own that they consider valid ways to improve the services provided? Are they comfortable with adopting practices and procedures that are introduced by researchers who are outside the workforce programs? Are they receptive to evaluators "looking over their shoulders" as they provide services? Can they take constructive criticism, if the intervention is shown not to work, and learn from the experience? In the same vein, can they learn from a successful intervention and implement continuous improvement?

In confronting these questions, successful engagement by WIBs and their staff first requires a culture that promotes and supports innovation, kindles a desire to find ways to improve services, embraces data-driven decisions, and accommodates a level of comfort with research methods. Staff must be willing to experiment with new ideas and approaches and accept the fact that not all ideas actually work. A culture that encourages risk taking may be counter to the culture to which many staff are accustomed. The workforce system has been subject to strict performance metrics since the days of the Job Training Partnership Act. Staffs from many WIBs are reluctant to try approaches that may cause them not to meet or exceed their performance targets. To overcome this hesitancy, a culture of innovation and risk taking must permeate the local organization. The board, leadership, and staff must be willing to take a chance on innovative ideas and communicate to others the same sentiment.

Second, local WIBs need support from state agencies that will encourage such a culture and provide the resources necessary to carry out such interventions. As for resources, RCT evaluations cannot be carried out without the proper data, and in many states the required data, such as UI wage records, are held closely by state agencies, which do not always share their data with local WIBs. Without access to UI wage records to track the employment outcomes of members of both the control and treatment groups, RCT—or any other evaluation methodology—is much more difficult and expensive to implement, if not impossible. Some states—Ohio, for example—have established a data clearinghouse in which researchers can access UI wage records and other administrative data to conduct evaluations and pursue pertinent research.[6] This arrangement in Ohio serves as an example for other states to follow.

Third, as much as possible, interventions need to be designed to be embedded seamlessly in the daily operations, and this includes the random-assignment component as well. Since in most cases these low-cost interventions are "nudges" and not radical changes in program offerings or in the delivery of services, the minimal disruption of operations for staff and customers helps to make participation more palatable.

Fourth, sponsors of low-cost interventions should be prepared to compensate local WIBs for their participation. Nevertheless, the fact that they are called "low-cost" means that few additional funds may be available for such a purpose. Ideally, a data-driven staff will see its engagement in innovative approaches as a way to improve outcomes, which could be considered incentive enough, particularly within a culture such as described above. The fact that WIOA is outcome based, research focused, and driven by objective metrics helps to promote such motivations.

Fifth, local WIBs (and state agencies) need access to talented researchers who can help design and then evaluate such interventions. Even if frontline staff have identified the intervention that they believe will improve customer service and program outcomes, researchers who are expert in the design and implementation of evaluations are needed to carry out the experiment.

RELEVANCE OF THE WORK-FIRST PILOT TO THE ADMINISTRATION'S GOALS FOR RCTs

The Upjohn Institute initiated the low-cost RCT described in this chapter long before the Obama administration directed federal agencies to pursue such interventions. In the late 1990s, the Institute received funding from the USDOL to defray the costs of housing, designing, conducting, and evaluating the intervention. The Institute was interested in carrying out such an experiment because of the Institute's unique marriage of research and operations. Having both functions together within one organization fosters a culture of innovation, experimentation, and evaluation, as described above. Other reasons for staff's willingness to participate in the pilot were the anticipated improvement in the operation of the program (such as improved handling of information and the targeted referrals of customers to services) and the minimal disruption to services since the intervention and evaluation were embedded in the operations.

The pilot program described here illustrates four aspects of the Obama administration's concept of low-cost RCTs. First, the pilot focuses on two of the four directives to federal agencies in the president's executive order: 1) improve how information is presented and 2) improve how choices of programs are presented to customers. The pilot streamlines the intake process by reducing the number of times participants must fill out registration forms, and it tries to match participants with providers that are better suited to respond to their specific needs. Second, part of the setup of this intervention was based on establishing an employability score, which was derived from statistical procedures similar to the profiling score required under Worker Profiling and Reemployment Services. Behavioral scientists, as reported in Babcock et al. (2012), advocate using profiling when assigning participants to various job search assistance services in order to minimize their procrastination in engaging in available programs. Third, the pilot embeds an RCT experiment directly in the intake process by randomly assigning participants (stratified by three levels of employability) to one of three service providers. Fourth, the RCT uses administrative data generated by the program to record participant characteristics and employment outcomes. This technique provides a low-cost evaluation instrument that can yield results in a short period of time.

Description of the Work First Pilot

The purpose of Michigan's Work First program was to move welfare recipients into jobs as quickly as possible. The program provided welfare recipients with reemployment skills, support, and opportunities to obtain employment, and it offered instruction in the proper techniques for writing résumés, completing applications, and interviewing for jobs. The purpose of the pilot was to improve the employment outcomes of participants in the state welfare-to-work program by streamlining the referral process so that services could be tailored to best meet the needs of participants.

At the time of the pilot, the Kalamazoo–St. Joseph Workforce Development Board contracted with three organizations to provide services under the Work First program. While each provider offered services required under the law, the three differed in their approach and in the mix of services provided. Institute staff administering the program observed that some participants responded more favorably to one approach than another, and they wanted to see if they could devise a system that would assign recipients to providers that best met their needs and in a style that best fit their personalities. The pilot referred welfare-to-work participants to one of three service providers based on a statistical algorithm that used administrative data to determine which provider offered services that were shown to be most effective for customers possessing specific characteristics and employment backgrounds. Prior to the pilot, participants were randomly assigned to providers. Information collected at that time was used to "teach" the referral algorithm which providers delivered the best outcomes for individuals with certain characteristics from each of the three employability groups. The pilot demonstrated that customizing services based on participant characteristics could increase the effectiveness and efficiency of the intervention. An RCT evaluation of the pilot demonstrated that customizing services based on participant characteristics could increase the effectiveness and efficiency of the program, as seen by an increase in the 90-day employment retention rate of participants and a benefit-cost ratio of three to one.

Description of the Referral Process

Institute staff worked closely with the local office of the state's social service agency, the Family Independence Agency, to administer the Work First program. The Family Independence Agency determined welfare eligibility, issued welfare payments, and referred welfare recipients to Work First programs, while the Work First agency provided welfare recipients with employment services through intermediaries.

The Family Independence Agency referred all qualified applicants to Work First within 10 days of their applying for cash assistance. Applicants were notified of the date and time they were to enroll in the program and attend orientation. Orientation included an introduction to the Work First program, specification of the roles and responsibilities of the program and client, and a brief assessment of the client's situation and immediate needs, including the possible need for supportive services. In-depth assessment and counseling were offered only to those in considerable need.

The Work First pilot incorporated a statistical assessment and referral system into the initial intake and orientation process. Each welfare recipient who enrolled in Work First was immediately assigned a score indicating his or her probability of finding employment. The score provided an assessment of each participant's need for services, based upon the past experiences of local Work First participants who had observable characteristics like that participant. A high score indicated that a person had little need of services, since past par-

ticipants with the same set of characteristics had shown a high probability of finding a job without much if any intervention. Those with
a low score required more services, since past recipients with similar
attributes had less success in finding and retaining employment. Each
participant was then referred to one of three subcontractors within
each of the employability scores.

Data were obtained from the intake forms and tracking system
developed and maintained by the Kalamazoo–St. Joseph Workforce
Development Board. By recording the type of activity, the number of
hours engaged in each activity, and the starting and ending dates of
each activity, it was possible to piece together a sequence of activities between the time participants entered and the time they left the
program.

Design of the Evaluation

The pilot was evaluated using a randomized controlled trial,
which was embedded in the intake process. The random-assignment
procedure took place in three steps. First, participants were divided
into one of three groups, depending upon their employability score.
Assignment of participants to the three employability groups was
based not on a predetermined cutoff value but on their ranking in the
distribution of employability scores of those who enrolled in Work
First at that session. Those participants with employability scores in
the lowest 40 percent of the distribution were assigned to the low
employability group (L), the next 20 percent were assigned to the
middle group (M), and the highest 40 percent were assigned to the
high group (H). The middle group included only 20 percent of the
participants since the treatment provider for that group could accommodate only that percentage of participants because of capacity
constraints.

Second, those within each employability group were randomly
divided between control and treatment groups of equal size. Third,
enrollees in the control group were randomly assigned to one of the

three providers. Those in the treatment group were assigned to a predetermined provider that the evidence showed to be most effective for those in one of the three employability groups. The evaluation included 3,600 welfare recipients who entered the Kalamazoo–St. Joseph Work First program from March 1998 to March 2000.

The primary outcome measure for the evaluation is the retention rate—that is, whether a participant was employed for 90 consecutive days after exiting the program. Table 3.1 shows the retention rates of those in the control and treatment groups by employability group and provider. In this case, there is considerable variation both across groups and within groups. Note that the actual retention rate averaged for each group increases from the lowest employability group to the highest. For the control group, it increases from 11.6 percent for the lowest group to 21.7 percent for the highest employability group. The treatment group also follows the pattern of exhibiting increased retention rates from low to high employability groups.

Retention Rates by Various Combinations of Providers

Three providers delivered services to the Work First participants in the pilot. It is obvious from Table 3.1 that the retention rates varied across employability groups and providers within those groups.

Table 3.1 Retention Rates, by Provider and Employability Group (%)

Employability groups	Low		Middle		High	
Control/treatment groups	Control	Treatment	Control	Treatment	Control	Treatment
Provider						
A	15.3	15.4	21.9		22.6	
B	7.9		14.5		22.3	23.4
C	13.6		37.0	17.0	16.7	
Average	11.6		20.8		21.7	

SOURCE: Author's calculations of Kalamazoo–St. Joseph Work First administrative data, 1996–1997.

To be more precise about the retention rates resulting from different combinations of providers, we examined six combinations of referrals. Since participants in the control group were randomly assigned to each of the three providers within each employability group, we used the retention rates for each group, as reported in Table 3.1, to compute the retention rates for each of the six combinations. The combinations are denoted in the following way: the letter refers to the provider, and its position in the combination of three letters refers to the assignment of participants from an employability group to that provider. For example, the first combination, acb, refers to members of the low employability group assigned to provider a, members of the middle employability group assigned to provider c, and members of the high employability group assigned to provider b.

Figure 3.1 displays the retention rates for the six groups, starting from the left with the combination yielding the highest retention rate and moving to the right with combinations yielding successively lower retention rates.[7] The difference between the retention rates of the highest-yielding combination (acb) and the combination with the lowest retention rate (bac) is 8.0 percentage points, and the difference between the combination with the highest retention rate and the retention rate if all participants were randomly assigned is 4.8 percentage points. Differences between any of the pairs of combinations are statistically significant at the 95 percent level.

BENEFIT-COST ANALYSIS OF THE STATISTICAL ASSESSMENT AND REFERRAL SYSTEM

The benefits of using the statistical assessment and referral system can be quantified by considering the earnings received by those additional participants who retained their jobs. As shown in the previous section, the optimal assignment rule yielded a net increase of 47 participants who retained their jobs for 90 consecutive days over the number retaining their jobs for that length of time in the group

**Figure 3.1 Retention Rates for Various Combinations of the Three
Providers According to Employability Group Assigned
to Them**

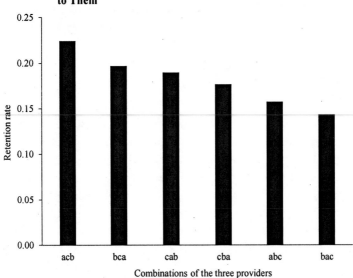

NOTE: In the *x* axis, the letters signifying providers a, b, and c have their order determined as follows: first letter = the provider to which the low employability group
is assigned; second letter = the provider to which the middle employability group
is assigned; third letter = the provider to which the high employability group is
assigned.
SOURCE: Author's compilation.

created by random assignment. Consequently, the net effect of the
statistical assessment and referral system is computed by considering
the difference in retention rates and earnings of the two groups. A
benefit-to-cost ratio is then calculated by dividing the net effect by the
cost of the pilot.[8] Two scenarios were considered. The first scenario
assumes that the difference in the number of participants retaining
their jobs for 90 days persists for eight quarters. The second scenario
assumes that the difference in job retention narrows throughout the
eight-quarter period until the two series are equal. In both scenarios,
wages are assumed to grow by 3 percent a year, and a 10 percent

annual discount rate is used when computing the net present value of the earnings streams. Dividing the net present value for each scenario by the program costs of $145,000 yields a benefit-to-cost ratio for the first scenario of 5.8 and a ratio for the second scenario of 3.3.[9]

SUMMARY

The potential of improving the effectiveness of social programs by incorporating behavioral insights into the delivery of services has received considerable attention among policymakers. The Obama administration encouraged federal agencies to find ways to improve programs through behavioral insights and established a special task force to help them with that effort. This chapter discusses how such efforts can become more widespread, particularly for programs that depend on a federal-state-local partnership to deliver services, such as is the case for the national workforce programs. The chapter offers the example of a USDOL-funded pilot conducted in the late 1990s as an illustration of how low-cost interventions in workforce programs can improve employment outcomes of participants. The pilot is relevant for the current interest in low-cost RCT experiments, in that it demonstrates how a simple improvement in the referral of participants to services can improve outcomes, how RCT can be embedded in the existing program, and how administrative data can be used to minimize the cost and disruption of the evaluation. It also illustrates the type of culture and the amount of resources needed for local WIBs to be willing to engage in such projects.

The Upjohn Institute conducted the pilot through its division that administers Work First programs and other workforce programs for the local workforce investment area. The unique organizational structure of the Institute, which combines both research and operations, perhaps offers some lessons of what it would take for other states and local WIBs to be able to undertake similar projects, short of establishing a similar organization. Based on the experience of conducting this pilot, one could conclude that for such ventures to be successful, it takes a culture of innovation, evidence-based decision making, the willingness to take some risks, and expertise in designing, implementing, and evaluating social experiments. The RCT showed that the pilot improved participants' employment outcomes with a benefit-cost ratio of greater than three to one.

The recent initiative for using low-cost interventions and RCTs to improve social programs came about from one administration's desire to improve the delivery of social services through insights gleaned from research in behavioral science. To sustain such efforts into the future, a culture of innovation, experimentation, and research must be embedded in the programs and the organizations responsible for administering those programs. The WIOA legislation, which governs the national workforce programs, codifies some aspects of a culture of innovation and assessment by requiring each state to evaluate the effectiveness of their programs on a regular basis using a rigorous methodology. It also mandates the use of a statistical methodology by states to adjust their performance targets.

For such legislation to nurture a culture throughout the system, there must be strong leadership at all three levels of the partnership—federal, state, and local—as well as a willingness to demonstrate flexibility. For example, the USDOL could be more willing to grant waivers to states and local WIBs to exempt them from meeting performance standards for short periods of time so they can pursue innovative ideas and approaches. States could demonstrate a willingness to support the pursuit of RCTs through making available the necessary data (e.g., UI wage records and other administrative records) and by creating an environment that encourages experimentation. Such an environment could be nurtured by offering forums for the exchange of ideas and creating a clearinghouse for the use of data. Finally, states and local WIBs could reach out to researchers from universities and other research organizations to partner on the design and evaluation of low-cost interventions.

Notes

1. Recently, the Behavioural Insights Team has evolved into a social purpose company and is no longer embedded in the Cabinet Office.
2. "Memorandum to the Heads of Departments and Agencies," Office of Management and Budget, July 2013.
3. One of the USDOL-sponsored "nudge" programs directed at workforce programs is being conducted at the Upjohn Institute through its division that administers WIOA programs for a four-county area in Southwest Michigan. The program was developed by frontline staff with the assistance of Ideas42 and Mathematica. It is being evaluated using an embedded RCT experiment.
4. The description of the pilot included in this chapter draws heavily from Eberts (2002).
5. SBST's website is inactive, suggesting that SBST has not been continued under the subsequent administration. A message at the top of the home page says, "This is historical material 'frozen in time' on January 20, 2017. This website will no longer be updated."
6. For an example, see www.ohioanalytics.gov.
7. More than six combinations are possible with three providers and three groups by assigning more than one employability group to a provider. However, we adhered to the workforce development board's contractual arrangement during the pilot that all three providers should deliver services. Therefore, we eliminated from consideration combinations that assigned two or three groups to one service provider.
8. The social value of the new system may be less than the value computed here because of displacement effects among the welfare population. It is conceivable that the additional retention by participants of the program with the new system may displace other welfare recipients from their existing jobs or preclude new Work First participants from finding jobs, since the additional retentions reduce the number of job vacancies.
9. The amount of $145,000 includes only the costs of developing and operating the statistical referral system over the two-year life of the pilot. It does not include the cost of providing the services once participants were referred to the providers.

References

Babcock, Linda, William J. Congdon, Lawrence F. Katz, and Sendhil Mullainathan. 2012. "Notes on Behavioral Economics and Labor Market Policy." *IZA Journal of Labor Policy* 1(2): 1–14.

Behavioural Insights Team. 2011. *Annual Update, 2010–2011*. London: UK Cabinet Office. https://www.gov.uk/government/uploads/system/uploads/attachment_data/file/60537/Behaviour-Change-Insight-Team-Annual-Update_acc.pdf (accessed April 21, 2017).

Eberts, Randall W. 2002. "Using Statistical Assessment Tools to Target Services to Work First Participants." In *Targeting Employment Services*, Randall W. Eberts, Christopher J. O'Leary, and Stephen A. Wandner, eds. Kalamazoo, MI: W.E. Upjohn Institute for Employment Research, pp. 221–244.

National Science and Technology Council. 2015. *Social and Behavioral Science Team: 2016 Annual Report*. Washington, DC: Executive Office of the President, National Science and Technology Council. https://sbst.gov/download/2015%20SBST%20Annual%20Report.pdf (accessed April 21, 2017).

———. 2016. *Social and Behavioral Science Team: 2016 Annual Report*. Washington, DC: Executive Office of the President, National Science and Technology Council. https://sbst.gov/download/2016%20SBST%20Annual%20Report.pdf (accessed April 21, 2017).

Shankar, Maya. 2014. "How Low-Cost Randomized Controlled Trials Can Drive Effective Social Spending." White House blog, July 30. https://obamawhitehouse.archives.gov/blog/2014/07/30/how-low-cost-randomized-controlled-trials-can-drive-effective-social-spending (accessed April 21, 2017).

Thaler, Richard H., and Cass R. Sunstein. 2008. *Nudge: Improving Decisions about Health, Wealth, and Happiness*. New Haven, CT: Yale University Press.

Wandner, Stephen A. 2010. *Solving the Reemployment Puzzle: From Research to Policy*. Kalamazoo, MI: W.E. Upjohn Institute for Employment Research.

White House. 2015. "Executive Order—Using Behavioral Science Insights to Better Serve the American People." Washington, DC: White House, Office of the Press Secretary. https://obamawhitehouse.archives.gov/the-press-office/2015/09/15/executive-order-using-behavioral-science-insights-better-serve-american (accessed April 21, 2017).

Chapter 4

Experimental Evaluations and the Evolution of the Reemployment and Eligibility Assessment Program

Jacob M. Benus

IMPAQ International

In 2005, the U.S. Department of Labor (USDOL) introduced the Reemployment and Eligibility Assessment (REA) Initiative, which provides grants to state workforce agencies to design and implement a new program to assist individuals claiming unemployment insurance (UI) benefits. The initiative began with $18 million in grants, which were distributed to 21 states and territories in Fiscal Year (FY) 2005. Since then, the REA program has grown to 44 states and an appropriation of $80 million in FY 2015.

In FY 2016, the Obama administration proposed an increase in funding of approximately $100 million to fund a combined Reemployment and Eligibility Assessment and Reemployment Services (REA/RES) program. If it is approved by the new administration, the proposed funding of $181 million would support an integrated approach for assisting unemployed workers to return to work more rapidly, thus reducing costs to the UI Trust Fund. The proposed budget request would provide funding for all states to serve the unemployed based on their projected number of targeted UI beneficiaries.

This chapter describes the evolution of the REA Initiative from a small experimental program designed to reduce UI expenditures to a permanent program that combines in-person eligibility reviews with reemployment services. The chapter begins with a description of the background of the conditions that led to the introduction of REA, fol-

61

lowed by a summary of prior research on the effectiveness of UI work search requirements and reemployment services. Next, the chapter presents the early history of the REA Initiative, its implementation, and the early research on the impact of REA. Finally, the chapter reviews the administration's new proposal for combining REA and RES and concludes with observations on the future of REA/RES.

BACKGROUND

The Social Security Act of 1935 and the Federal Unemployment Tax Act of 1939 established the current federal-state system for providing temporary and partial wage replacement benefits for covered and eligible unemployed workers. Since then, the unemployment insurance system has evolved dramatically as the number of beneficiaries has grown over time and as new technologies for administering the program have been developed and implemented.

In the early years of the UI program, unemployed individuals were required to apply for unemployment benefits in person. In recent years, states have modernized and automated the procedures for applying for and receiving UI benefits. In 2005, for example, 44 states accepted initial claims for unemployment insurance by telephone or the Internet (GAO 2005). Today, only three states (Arkansas, Vermont, and West Virginia) do not accept initial UI applications filed on the Internet. All other states accept initial and continuing claims remotely. As a result, in many states it is currently possible for a claimant to file an initial claim and continue to claim benefits without speaking to anyone in person.

AUTOMATION AND DECLINE IN FUNDING FOR ADMINISTRATION OF UI

The secretary of labor is charged with providing funds to states for "proper and efficient administration" of state UI programs. These administrative funds are used by states to ensure that claimants are "monetarily" and "nonmonetarily" eligible to receive UI benefits and to refer beneficiaries to job search assistance provided at American Job Centers (formerly known as One-Stop Career Centers).

While past research has shown that connecting UI claimants with job opportunities early in their unemployment spell is highly effective in promoting reemployment, a number of factors in the 1990s led to a growing disconnect between the UI benefits program and the reemployment services programs. One source of this disconnect was the elimination of in-person applications for UI benefits. That is, in the early days of the UI program, claimants had to come to a local office to apply for benefits. The advent of telephone call centers in the 1990s and the introduction of Internet applications eliminated the need and opportunities for claimants to have any in-person interactions with a claims taker or job placement counselor.

Another source of disconnect between the UI benefits and reemployment services programs has been the gradual reduction in the use of the Eligibility Review Program (ERP) since the 1980s. Under the ERP, UI beneficiaries were required to report that they remained eligible and were continuing to search for work. Over time, the use of ERPs declined—further disconnecting the UI program from opportunities to connect unemployed individuals to employment services.

In tandem with the increase in automation and the decline in the use of ERPs, funding for administering the UI system declined in real terms. Today, funding for administering the UI system (in constant terms) is lower than it was in the 1980s. With insufficient funds for the "proper and efficient administration" of state UI programs, the federal government has often provided supplemental funding for administering the UI program through various mechanisms, including grants for information technology modernization. The introduction of the REA Initiative in 2005 may be viewed as a mechanism for enhancing funding for UI administration by supporting activities to enhance the integrity of UI payments. That is, by providing states with REA grants, the federal government was providing funds for conducting eligibility reviews, which had declined in previous years because of budget constraints.

PRIOR RESEARCH ON UI WORK SEARCH REQUIREMENTS

There is a rich literature on the effectiveness of UI work search requirements, employment services, and the combination of work search and employment services. For a complete review of this literature, see Wandner (2010). Below, we summarize some of the key studies that evaluated the effectiveness of alternative work search requirements.

One of the earliest studies to investigate the work search requirement was the Charleston Claimant Placement and Work Test Demonstration (Corson, Long, and Nicholson 1985). This 1983 study randomly assigned UI beneficiaries to three treatment groups: 1) enhanced work test, 2) special employment services, and 3) job search workshop. The enhanced work test group was required to come in to the office to register for work and was subject to termination from UI if its members did not register. The treatment was found to be effective and reduced UI duration by more than a half week of benefits.

The Washington Alternative Work Search Experiment was implemented in 1986 and 1987 in Tacoma, Washington (Johnson and Klepinger 1991). The experiment tested the effect of altering the number of employer contacts required for continuing eligibility. The experiment had three treatment groups: for the first group, the experiment eliminated the reporting of employer contacts; for the second group, it varied the number of employer contacts over time; and for the third group, it retained the required contacts and added employment services early in the unemployment spell. The main finding of this study was that the elimination of the reporting requirement significantly increased the duration of benefits. Without a need to report employer contacts, beneficiaries collected three weeks' more benefits than those who *were* required to report employer contacts. Thus, the conclusion from this study is that the integrity of the UI system is affected by the work search requirement.

The Maryland UI Work Search Demonstration was conducted in 1994–1995 to test alternative work search requirements (Klepinger et al. 1998). In this experimental design evaluation, UI beneficiaries were randomly assigned to either a control group that continued the normal practice or one of four treatment groups: 1) a group that continued the normally required two employer work-search contacts and offered a job search workshop, 2) a group that increased the required number of employer work search contacts from two to four a week, 3) a group that supplemented the normal two-employer work-search requirement with information about verification of employer contacts, and 4) a group that did not require claimants to document their employer contacts. The evaluation found that offering the job search workshop (Treatment 1) reduced the duration of UI benefits by 0.6 weeks. Increasing the required work search contacts from two to four employer contacts a week (Treatment 2) reduced the duration of UI benefits by 0.7 weeks. Informing claimants that their employer contacts might be verified (Treatment 3) had a similar impact—it reduced the duration of UI benefits by 0.9 weeks. Finally, not requiring claimants to document their employer contacts (Treatment 4) had the opposite impact—it increased the duration of benefits by 0.4 weeks. This last result was confirmed by a similar finding in a study in Northern Ireland (McVicar 2010).

In addition to these studies on the impact of alternative work search requirements, there have been numerous studies to assess the impact of job search assistance and other reemployment services.

These studies—e.g., the National Worker Profiling and Reemployment Services Evaluation (Dickinson et al. 1999), the Kentucky Worker Profiling and Reemployment Services Evaluation (Black et al. 2003), and the Eight State WIA Implementation Study (Barnow and King 2005)—have consistently found significant reductions in the duration of UI benefits when reemployment services are offered. There is, however, substantial variation across these studies resulting from the differences across states in the reemployment services provided.

Currently, USDOL's Chief Evaluation Office is supporting a random-assignment evaluation of REA that is designed to isolate the impact of the two major components of the REA/RES program: 1) the in-person employment eligibility review and 2) reemployment services. This study may shed light on the relative impact of the two major components of the program and the interaction between these components.

EARLY HISTORY OF REA INITIATIVE

The REA Initiative was introduced by USDOL in 2005 as a new approach that combines in-person UI eligibility reviews with the provision of labor market information and referral to reemployment services (USDOL 2005). While the REA Initiative began in 2005, its features are grounded in past research findings and proven methods of administration that have been shown to be efficient and cost effective. Below, we present the precursor programs that helped to shape the 2005 REA features. A complete history of these precursor programs can be found in Wandner (2010).

Beginning in the 1940s, states established rules to require that claimants provide evidence of work search contacts. Furthermore, some states implemented periodic reviews of claimants' work search efforts after a specified number of weeks. By the late 1960s, the periodic review of eligibility was being tested with different combinations of job finding, placement services, and training in a series of research demonstrations. In the 1970s, research findings were incorporated into a national design of the Eligibility Review Program. The purpose of this program was to help states to reestablish sound eligibility review processes in the UI program.

Starting in the early 1990s, states began to implement cost-efficient self-service claims-taking and job-finding-and-placement systems. In the next few years, many states automated their UI systems so that initial and continued claims could be filed through touch-tone telephones or the Internet. Using these automated systems, claimants were able to respond to questions about their job search by pressing or entering "yes" or "no" to standardized questions. This increased automation, together with the relocation of UI staff to call and data centers, has caused some claimants to become detached from the local American Job Centers delivery system.

In the early 2000s, policymakers recognized that greater attention should be directed to the continued eligibility review process and the reemployment needs of UI claimants. As a result, in March 2005, USDOL funded a total of 21 states to provide in-person interviews and other services to individuals claiming UI benefits through the REA program. The early design of REA required states to select a portion of their UI beneficiaries to attend one-on-one interviews in person. These interviews included a review of ongoing UI eligibility, provision of current labor market information, development of a work search plan, and referral to reemployment services and training, as needed.

EVALUATIONS OF THE REA INITIATIVE

Soon after USDOL's selection of the grantees, IMPAQ International was asked by USDOL to provide grantees with technical assistance. This technical assistance to grantees covered both 1) assistance in the development of rigorous random-assignment procedures for assigning UI beneficiaries to treatment and control groups and 2) assistance in collecting and reporting accurate information on reemployment. This technical assistance was critical to the early development of the REA Initiative since, initially, USDOL provided only the following five broad guidelines for implementing the REA Initiative (USDOL 2004):

1) Funds may be used only for in-person reemployment and eligibility assessments for UI beneficiaries that are conducted in One-Stop facilities.

2) Assessments must include labor-market information/ work-search plan development/review, referral to employment services and to training when appropriate, and eligibility issue detection and referral to adjudication when appropriate.

3) Grantees must agree to participate in a USDOL-funded study of the efficacy of the UI REA Initiative.

4) Beneficiaries must report in person to the One-Stop Center within a specified period of time as part of the assessment.

5) Assessments were to be conducted only for claimants who did not have a definite return-to-work date.

Within these general parameters, grantees had a great deal of leeway in designing their state REA programs. As a result of this flexibility, the programs varied dramatically across the 21 grantees. For example, some grantees implemented their program statewide, while other grantees implemented their program in selected areas of the state. The greatest variation, however, was in how states selected UI beneficiaries into a treatment group (those who received REA services) and a control group (those who received no REA services). For example, some grantees did not understand the requirement for rigorous random assignment. Others understood the requirement but did not have a computerized random-assignment process and used inappropriate random-assignment procedures. Still others selected treatment and control groups from different populations, resulting in unequal treatment and control groups. As a result of these difficulties and deficient random-assignment procedures, in some states it was impossible to measure program effectiveness by comparing outcomes of the resulting treatment and control groups.

TECHNICAL ASSISTANCE AND EVALUATION OF THE 2005 REA INITIATIVE

IMPAQ began providing technical assistance to grantees in June 2005. As part of this technical assistance project, IMPAQ analyzed the early implementation of nine states' REA programs. This implementation analysis revealed that, for the most part, the services provided to participants followed the general guidelines established by the Employment and Training Administration. That is, states were successful in conducting in-person REA sessions that combined verification of continued eligibility for UI benefits with referral to reemployment services. However, the analysis also revealed that states had difficulty in complying with the requirements to develop an appropriate methodology for three aspects: 1) selecting treatment and comparison groups, 2) collecting outcomes data for the treatment and comparison groups, and 3) submitting accurate data to USDOL.

IMPAQ's implementation analysis of nine states revealed that several states were not able to accurately implement the required random-assignment procedures. In addition, states had difficulty in collecting and reporting accurate outcome information for the selected treatment and control group members. For example, several states indicated that they would be delayed or entirely unable to submit the two required outcome reports: 1) the ETA 9128 Reemployment and Eligibility Assessment Activities report and 2) the ETA 9129 Reemployment and Eligibility Assessment Outcomes report. As a result of these difficulties, an alternative methodology was developed to assess the early impacts of the REA program.

Since states were unable to provide the required data to assess program impacts, IMPAQ and ETA developed an alternative methodology for assessing the effectiveness of the REA Initiative. Specifically, IMPAQ developed a methodology that used state UI administrative records and follow-up interview data to assess REA effectiveness. This approach was used in evaluating REA effectiveness in two states that had designed and implemented rigorous random-assignment procedures—Minnesota and North Dakota (Benus et al. 2008). We describe these impact assessments below.

Minnesota implemented the REA Initiative in 12 One-Stop Career Centers. Since Wagner-Peyser Act funds were already available to serve claimants whose profiling scores were high (i.e., those in the top third), Minnesota designed its REA Initiative to serve the middle third of profiled claimants. Thus, the Minnesota REA Initiative did not serve claimants who were the most likely to exhaust their UI benefits or the least likely to exhaust UI benefits; rather, the Minnesota program was designed to serve those in the middle.

For this target population, Minnesota designed a rigorous random-assignment process. Individuals were randomly assigned to either a control group (no REA services) or to one of two treatment groups:

- T1: single REA interview group—members were required to attend one in-person interview, or

- T2: multiple REA interviews group—members were required to attend more than one in-person interview.

Using UI administrative data and follow-up interview data, the study results indicated that the T1 group (single REA) did not have a significant impact on most UI-related outcomes (e.g., weeks claimed and weeks compensated). Nonetheless, the T1 group did exhibit a reduction in the likelihood of overpayment by 3.5 percentage points. This statistically significant result is similar to the reduction in the likelihood of overpayments for T2 (3.8 percentage points). Since the T1 and T2 groups received the same REA letter, this result suggests that the letter itself may have had an impact on reducing overpayments.

For the T2 group (multiple REAs), unlike the T1 group, REA services did have statistically significant impacts on UI-related outcomes. Specifically, regression-adjusted impact estimates indicate that multiple REAs significantly reduce the following:

- the number of weeks claimed (0.9 weeks)
- the number of weeks claimed and compensated (1.2 weeks)
- the likelihood of exhausting UI benefits (3.7 percentage points)
- the likelihood of having an overpayment (3.8 percentage points)

The REA Initiative in North Dakota was implemented in five One-Stop Career Centers. Since non-job-attached UI claimants were already required to participate in eligibility reviews and to receive reemployment services, the introduction of REA did not dramatically alter existing services. Using UI administrative data and follow-up interview data, the study found no statistically significant impact of REA. These results are not surprising, since control group members in North Dakota received similar, but less intensive, services than treatment group members. The lack of statistically significant impacts may also be due to the limited size of the North Dakota sample.

FOUR-STATE EVALUATION OF THE REA INITIATIVE

In 2008, USDOL asked IMPAQ to assess REA program impacts during the period from July 2009 to December 2009. The study included process and impact analyses of REA programs in four states: Florida, Idaho, Illinois, and Nevada (Poe-Yamagata et al. 2011). The process analysis revealed the following results:

- All states conducted in-person interviews as required by their REA grants.

- All states referred to adjudication those claimants who did not participate in the REA interview.

- All states reported the data on their REA implementation to USDOL; however, states had difficulty in meeting the requirement to report REA program impacts.

- States differed in staff assignment to REA. Some REA interviewers devoted 100 percent of their time to REA; other interviewers spent only a portion of their time on REA and the remainder on other activities.

- States differed in determining REA eligibility. Some selected claimants for REA services based on their likelihood of exhausting UI benefits. Others selected only those with work experience in a high-demand occupation.

- In some states, REA interviews were conducted as early as four weeks after the initial claim-filing date, and in other states as late as eight weeks.

- Rescheduling of REA appointments was generally permitted; however, there was substantial variation in how many times a claimant could reschedule.

- In most states, REA interviewers referred claimants to reemployment services and training. In Nevada, the REA program and the RES program were fully integrated.

The impact evaluation addressed the following key research questions:

- Did REA lead to a reduction in benefit exhaustion, UI claim duration, and total UI benefits?

- Did REA lead to savings for the UI Trust Fund?

- Did REA lead to savings after deducting REA program costs?

- Was REA effective in assisting UI recipients to become reemployed?

States were required to randomly assign UI claimants into either a treatment group or a control group to evaluate the effectiveness of the REA Initiative. Treatment group members were required to participate in REA services; control group members were not required to do so. While the random-assignment process differed somewhat across the study states, the four states selected for this study all had rigorous random-assignment designs that yielded treatment and control groups that were similar on all characteristics. The impact results in each of the four study states follow.

Florida Impact Results

- REA led to significant reductions in the duration of receiving regular UI and extended unemployment compensation (EUC) benefits. On average, REA claimants received 1.74 fewer weeks of benefits compared to the control group.

- REA participants experienced a significant reduction (3.4 percentage points) in the likelihood of exhausting regular benefits and a significant reduction (3.3 percentage points) in the likelihood of receiving EUC benefits.

- The REA program, on average, reduced total regular UI benefits by $101 and extended benefit payments by $294. Combining the reductions in regular UI benefits and extended benefits, REA reduced total benefits by $395, on average.

- The combined $395 reduction in benefit amounts received per treatment group member greatly exceeded the estimated $54 cost per treatment group member.[1]

- REA had positive impacts on reemployment outcomes, as estimated by earnings in the four quarters following the start of the UI claim. REA treatment group members had higher wages ($476 more) than their control group peers in the four quarters following the start of their UI claim.

Idaho Impact Results

- REA led to a significant reduction in the duration of receiving regular UI and EUC benefits. On average, REA claimants received 1.14 fewer weeks of benefits than the control group.

- REA participants experienced a significant reduction (3.2 percentage points) in the likelihood of exhausting regular benefits and a significant reduction (3.1 percentage points) in the likelihood of receiving extended benefits.

- REA reduced total benefit amounts received by $262 per REA participant. On average, REA participants received $97 less in regular UI benefits and $165 less in extended benefits than control group members.

- In Idaho, all treatment group members received an REA letter. The letter required participants to complete an online REA questionnaire. The average cost per REA participant was $12. Those who did not complete the questionnaire were referred to adjudication. Among those who did complete the questionnaire, a random sample were invited to participate in an in-person REA interview.

- Inasmuch as the per-claimant savings of the REA program amounted to $262, the savings substantially exceeded the cost per treatment group member.

Illinois Impact Results

There is no evidence that the Illinois REA program led to changes in the duration of receiving regular UI or extended benefits, in the likelihood of regular UI benefit exhaustion or receipt of extended benefits, or in the amount of benefit receipt.

The lack of significant impact findings in Illinois may be attributed to several factors:

- There was a lack of consistency in the implementation of the program:
  - the REA program was suspended in December 2008, and
  - the REA program was restarted in June 2009 (just prior to the start of the study period).
- Both groups had a small sample size (only 2,175 in the treatment group, and only 937 in the control group).
- The REA program design targeted claimants with high-demand skills, thus restricting the population eligible for REA selection.

Nevada Impact Results

REA led to significant reductions in the duration of UI benefits. On average, REA claimants received 2.96 fewer weeks of benefits compared to their control group peers.

REA participants experienced a significant reduction (10.4 percentage points) in the likelihood of exhausting regular benefits and a significant reduction (9.0 percentage points) in the likelihood of receiving extended benefits.

On average, REA reduced total benefit amounts received by $805. REA participants received, on average, $526 less in regular UI benefits and $279 less in extended benefits than control group members.

The average cost per REA participant was $53. However, since REA and RES services and funding were so closely integrated, we combined the average costs of providing the integrated REA and RES. The estimated combined cost was $201 per REA treatment group member. The reduction in total benefit amounts received was $805 per treatment group member, which greatly exceeds the combined REA and RES costs.

The results of this analysis of REA program impacts indicate that the REA program was effective in assisting claimants in Florida, Idaho, and Nevada to exit the UI program and avoid exhausting regular UI benefits. There was no impact in Illinois; however, the Illinois REA program suffered from inconsistent implementation, small sample size, and restricting the program to claimants with high-demand skills.

By enabling claimants to avoid UI benefit exhaustion, the program led to reductions in the likelihood of their receiving EUC benefits. The combined impacts of reducing program exhaustion and reducing receipt of EUC benefits led to significantly shorter UI durations and lower benefit amounts. Furthermore, the reductions in benefits substantially exceeded the per-participant REA cost in the states. These results provide strong evidence that the REA program is a cost-effective program.

A key finding of our analysis is that there were substantially larger impacts in Nevada than in the other study states. While other states referred many REA participants to reemployment services, Nevada provided reemployment services to REA treatment group members in conjunction with the REA interview. It appears likely that Nevada's combination of REA services with RES led to the greater program impacts.

Based on the results of this analysis, we conclude that the REA program is an effective strategy for facilitating the exit of UI claimants from the UI program and for producing savings. Furthermore, the results suggest that combining REA services with RES into a seamless delivery system may achieve greater impacts than providing REA services alone.

EVALUATION OF THE NEVADA REA INITIATIVE

The 2011 evaluation of the impact of REA found evidence that the REA program was effective at achieving the program's goals of reducing UI duration and generating savings to the UI Trust Fund. An important finding of this study was that the Nevada REA program was more effective at reducing claimant UI duration and generating greater savings for the UI Trust Fund than the REA programs in the other states examined. The implementation of Nevada's REA program differed from the implementation in other states. In Nevada, the same staff provided both REA and RES.[2] In the other three study states, different staff administered REA and RES. It appears that providing REA and RES by the same staff in a single integrated session may be a key factor that led to greater program impacts in Nevada.

In light of these findings, USDOL asked IMPAQ to extend the study of the Nevada REA program using updated data on UI receipt and wages for REA-eligible claimants who entered the program from July through December of 2009. This follow-up study (Michaelides et al. 2012) used Nevada's administrative UI data and intrastate wage records for all REA-eligible UI claimants who entered the program during this six-month period. These sources provided the following data:

- UI receipt from program entry through September 2011
- quarterly wages earned in the six calendar quarters after program entry

Using these data, the evaluation assessed the impact of the Nevada REA program on claimant UI receipt and quarterly wage outcomes following program entry. The analysis found that the Nevada REA program was effective at assisting claimants to exit the UI program sooner than they would have in the absence of the program, leading to lower UI duration and producing important savings for the UI Trust Fund. The analysis also found that the program was effective in helping claimants find employment in the period following program entry. Based on these results, the researchers concluded that the Nevada REA program is an effective policy tool for reducing UI duration and assisting UI claimants to return to productive employment more rapidly than they would in the absence of the program.

The Nevada study extends the earlier study of the Nevada REA program using updated data on UI receipt and wages for REA-eligible claimants who entered the UI program from July through

December of 2009. During this period, Nevada randomly assigned about 15 percent of REA-eligible claimants to the treatment group. These claimants were required to receive REA services and reemployment services to remain eligible for UI benefits. The remaining 85 percent of REA-eligible claimants were assigned to the control group and were not required to receive any services.

Results of the analysis from the earlier study, like the later one, showed that the Nevada REA program was effective in helping claimants to exit the UI program sooner. The analysis also shows that claimants in the REA treatment group were significantly less likely than those in the control group to exhaust regular UI benefits and start receiving extended benefits. Thus, the Nevada REA program led to significantly shorter UI durations and lower benefit amounts—REA treatment group claimants collected 3.13 fewer weeks and $873 less in total benefit amounts than their peers. These savings exceeded average program costs by more than four times, providing strong evidence that the Nevada REA program is a cost-effective intervention.

The impact analyses also show that the Nevada REA program was effective in assisting claimants to obtain employment in the first two quarters following program entry. Furthermore, these impacts were sustained through six quarters following program entry. Because of these impacts, REA treatment group members returned to employment faster than their peers, which led to their earning higher total wages following program entry. These results suggest that, in addition to assisting claimants in exiting UI early, REA helped claimants to obtain employment earlier than they would have in the absence of the program.

Overall, these impact analyses provide strong evidence that the Nevada REA program is an effective strategy for facilitating the exit of UI claimants from the UI program and producing savings for the UI Trust Fund. It is also evident that the program is effective in facilitating the reemployment of UI claimants. Based on these results, the authors concluded that Nevada's system of combining REA services with RES into a seamless delivery system is an effective mechanism for reducing UI duration and for assisting claimants to return to productive employment.

While the Nevada results indicate that combining REA with RES is highly effective in returning unemployed workers to employment, it would be of interest to determine the relative importance of REA and RES. To isolate the effect of REA and RES, one would need to develop a random-assignment study where eligible claimants would be assigned to different combinations of REA and RES.

EVOLUTION OF REA INTO RESEA

Based on the strong Nevada findings, USDOL has recently proposed significant increases in program funding as well as dramatic changes to the design of the UI REA program. One indication of the changes that are taking place is the change in program name. In 2015, USDOL changed the name of the program from Reemployment and Eligibility Assessment (REA) to Reemployment Services and Eligibility Assessment (RESEA). This name change reinforces the increasing emphasis of the program on reemployment services.

The program name change, together with a proposed increase of $100 million in funding (to $180.9 million), is expected to have dramatic impacts on future operations of the program. Funding for the program has grown dramatically since its inception in 2005.

As program services and the target population are expanded under the RESEA program, funding will likely continue to grow in future years. For example, the new RESEA funds may be used to provide reemployment services to program participants; previously, UI REA program funds could be used only for referrals to reemployment services. Furthermore, the target population for the RESEA program includes both UI claimants who are identified as likely to exhaust benefits and in need of reemployment services and claimants receiving unemployment compensation for ex–service members. Thus, a portion of the RESEA funds will be used to provide reemployment services to all recently separated military personnel receiving ex-service-member benefits.

With these proposed changes, REA and RES will no longer be disconnected; rather, they will be closely integrated into a single program. USDOL's budget justification for an increased budget of $100 million and for combining REA and RES into a single RESEA program is based largely on the successful model established in Nevada (USDOL 2016). In fact, the features of the new RESEA program are similar to the Nevada program:

- in-person interviews to review eligibility for UI benefits

- provision of labor market and career information to claimants to inform their career choices

- support for the development of a reemployment and work search plan

- orientation to services available through American Job Centers

- provision of staff-assisted reemployment services, including skills assessment, career counseling, job matching and referrals, job search assistance workshops, and referrals to training, as appropriate

CONCLUSION

The development of the REA program owes a great deal to prior studies on the effectiveness of four aspects: 1) job search assistance, 2) work search requirements, 3) reemployment services, and 4) the combination of work search and employment services. Findings from this research led USDOL to develop the basic parameters of the REA Initiative.

Since its introduction in 2005, the REA Initiative has evolved dramatically—from a small experimental program that covered only a few states to a large program that covers nearly all states. Moreover, the focus of the program has changed. In its early years, it focused on identifying fraud and abuse, reducing UI benefit duration, and generating savings for the UI Trust Fund. In more recent years, USDOL has shifted the emphasis and encouraged states to provide additional reemployment services, including skills assessments, career counseling, job matching and referrals, job search assistance workshops, and referrals to training, as appropriate.

This evolution of the REA program may be attributed, at least partly, to the research findings of several REA evaluations. In particular, the positive impacts found in the evaluation of the Nevada REA program led to a dramatic shift in program design to integrate reemployment services with the early focus on eligibility assessment. The evolution of the REA program could not have occurred without the ongoing support of USDOL for evaluating the impacts of the program and for identifying the underlying mechanism that generated these impacts.

The experiences of the REA Initiative can inform future USDOL programs designed to assist unemployed workers in returning to work. For example, providing states with implementation flexibility can be very beneficial. In the REA Initiative, grantees were given wide latitude in designing their state's program. This variation across states provided researchers with a rich array of program designs to compare. One of these designs (Nevada's) proved to be highly effective and therefore a candidate for emulation in other states.

Another lesson learned from the experiences of the REA Initiative is that most states do not have the skills or resources needed to conduct a rigorous impact evaluation, as is mentioned in the Eberts chapter of this volume. To enable them to do so, USDOL should engage outside technical assistance to ensure that random assignment is conducted accurately and that program effectiveness is measured rigorously.

Thus, the basic lesson learned from the REA study is that states are often in the best position to design programs that work best in their environment. At the same time, states often do not have the skills or resources to rigorously measure program effectiveness without significant outside expertise.

Notes

1. The average cost per treatment group member is derived by dividing the state's grant amount by the number of REAs conducted in the state.
2. The Nevada REA approach is similar to a 1970s experiment funded and implemented by the Nevada state workforce agency, but there is no evidence that the Nevada staff implementing the REA experiment were aware of the earlier Nevada experiment.

References

Barnow, Burt S., and Christopher T. King. 2005. *The Workforce Investment Act in Eight States*. Washington, DC: US Department of Labor, Employment and Training Administration.

Benus, Jacob, Eileen Poe-Yamagata, Ying Wang, and Etan Blass. 2008. "Reemployment Eligibility Assessment (REA) Study: FY2005 Initiative." Final Report. ETA Occasional Paper 2008-02. Washington, DC: U.S. Department of Labor, Employment and Training Administration.

Black, Dan A., Jeffrey A. Smith, Mark C. Berger, and Brett J. Noel. 2003. "Is the Threat of Reemployment Services More Effective than the Services Themselves? Evidence from Random Assignment in the UI System." *American Economic Review* 93(4): 1313–1327.

Corson, Walter, David Long, and Walter Nicholson. 1985. "Evaluation of the Charleston Claimant Placement and Work Test Demonstration." Department of Labor Unemployment Insurance Occasional Paper. Princeton, NJ: Mathematica Policy Research.

Dickinson, Katherine P., Paul T. Decker, Suzanne D. Kreutzer, and Richard W. West. 1999. *Evaluation of Worker Profiling and Reemployment Services: Final Report*. Research and Evaluation Report Series 99–D. Washington, DC: U.S. Department of Labor, Employment and Training Administration, Office of Policy and Research.

Government Accountability Office (GAO). 2005. *Unemployment Insurance: Better Data Needed to Assess Reemployment Services to Claimants.* Report to the Chairman, Subcommittee on Human Resources, Committee on Ways and Means, House of Representatives. GAO-05-413. Washington, DC: U.S. Government Accountability Office.

Johnson, Terry R., and Daniel H. Klepinger. 1991. "Evaluation of the Impacts of the Washington Alternative Work Search Experiment." Unemployment Insurance Occasional Paper No. 91-4. Washington, DC: U.S. Department of Labor, Employment and Training Administration.

Klepinger, Daniel H., Terry R. Johnson, Jutta M. Joesch, and Jacob M. Benus. 1998. "Evaluation of the Maryland Unemployment Insurance Work Search Demonstration." Unemployment Insurance Occasional Paper No. 98-2. Washington, DC: U.S. Department of Labor, Employment and Training Administration.

McVicar, Duncan, 2010. "Does Job Search Monitoring Intensity Affect Unemployment? Evidence from Northern Ireland." *Economica* 77(306): 296–313.

Michaelides, Marios, Eileen Poe-Yamagata, Jacob Benus, and Dharmendra Tirumalasetti. 2012. *Impact of the Reemployment and Eligibility Assessment (REA) Initiative in Nevada.* Columbia, MD: Impaq International. http://www.impaqint.com/sites/default/files/project-reports/ETAOP_2012_08_REA_Nevada_Follow_up_Report.pdf (accessed April 26, 2017).

Poe-Yamagata, Eileen, Jacob Benus, Nicholas Bill, Hugh Carrington, Marios Michaelides, and Ted Shen. 2011. *Impact of the Reemployment and Eligibility Assessment (REA) Initiative.* Final Report to Congress. Columbia, MD: Impaq International.

U.S. Department of Labor (USDOL). 2004. *Region 5 ETA Workforce Development Letter No. 013-04.* Washington, DC: U.S. Department of Labor, Employment and Training Administration. http://www.doleta.gov/regions/reg05/documents/WDL013-04.cfm (accessed July 18, 2017).

———. 2005. "U.S. Secretary of Labor Elaine L. Chao Announces Nearly $18 Million in New Reemployment and Eligibility Assessment Grants." News release, March 10. Washington, DC: U.S. Department of Labor. http://www.dol.gov/opa/media/press/opa/archive/OPA20050343.htm (accessed August 21, 2017).

———. 2016. *State Unemployment Insurance and Employment Ser-*

vice Operations. FY 2016 Congressional Budget Justification. Washington, DC: U.S. Department of Labor, Employment and Training Administration. https://www.dol.gov/sites/default/files/ documents/general/budget/2016/CBJ-2016-V1-09.pdf (accessed April 26, 2017).

Wandner, Stephen A. 2010. *Solving the Reemployment Puzzle: From Research to Policy*. Kalamazoo: W.E. Upjohn Institute for Employment Research.

Chapter 5

Incentive Experiments in Unemployment Insurance

Christopher J. O'Leary

W.E. Upjohn Institute for Employment Research

Unemployment insurance was established to provide partial temporary income replacement during periods of active job search by involuntarily unemployed labor force members. The program has achieved that objective faithfully since 1937. However, economic theory suggests that paying unemployment insurance (UI) benefits may prolong joblessness, and econometric research has found evidence that UI work disincentives do exist. This led to a series of randomized controlled trials to identify ways to overcome work disincentives while still paying UI. The experiments have assessed interventions on both sides of the job market. Job seeker trials have tested cash reemployment incentives in various ways: by monitoring active work search, by trying new types of job search assistance, by checking UI benefit eligibility, and by targeting assistance based on worker characteristics. Employer trials have tested hiring incentive payments, self-employment assistance, and ways to encourage work sharing. This chapter reviews the experimental evidence and considers it in the current context of the federal-state UI system.

POLICY BACKGROUND

Policies to support labor markets in the United States are mostly initiatives of the federal government. Historically, states have been reluctant to independently pursue public employment policy for fear of competitively disadvantaging resident industries with added costs.

Federal requirements and funding have allowed the states to address labor market problems with a diminished risk of job loss from interstate competition for jobs.

The Wagner-Peyser Act of 1933 established the U.S. Employment Service (ES), and the Social Security Act of 1935 established the federal-state UI system. These New Deal programs are at the core of federal employment policy, and they have evolved over time, as was described in the previous chapter. Since the 1980s, the states have truly served as laboratories of democracy, testing promising policy improvements by running classical field experiments with randomized controlled trials on large samples of program-eligible persons.

This chapter summarizes the lessons learned from UI experiments conducted in states over the past 35 years. To set the stage for this discussion, the next section briefly reviews the principles and pitfalls of evaluation with experiments that were discussed in greater depth in Chapter 2 of this book. The subsequent sections summarize evidence from experiments in the ES-UI context that have been done to identify ways to promote employment and conserve UI reserves. The concluding section of this chapter offers a summary and some comments on the relevance of lessons from these experiments for the UI system today.

THE APPEAL OF FIELD EXPERIMENTS

Classically designed field experiments involving randomized controlled trials (RCTs) are the gold standard for estimating the impact of changes to public programs. If random assignment is achieved, modeling of behavior and complex econometric methods are not needed to obtain reliable program impact estimates.[1] With large samples randomly assigned to treatment and control groups, observable and unobservable characteristics of the two groups should not differ on average, so any difference in outcomes can be attributed to the program change. Average program impacts can be measured as the simple difference between the means of the samples of program participants and of control group members on outcomes of interest. Since this process is easy to understand, impact estimates computed in this way can be influential for public policy.[2]

Policy decisions about whether to continue, expand, reduce, or cancel government employment programs require estimates of the net benefits from government spending. Cost-benefit analysis requires measurement of net program impacts, and such evaluations are not without potential problems—even if the evaluation is done under the ideal conditions of a field experiment. The first potential pitfall threatens the *internal validity* of the experiment. Such problems include errors in random assignment and changing experimental conditions. The first of these can lead to lack of balance in characteristics between treatment and control groups. The second means that the same trial was not successfully repeated in all cases. Even with internally valid randomization, problems can result from dropout bias (wherein a customer assigned to an experimental treatment did not in fact receive the service) and substitution bias (wherein a control group member actually receives the treatment) (Heckman et al. 2000).

The second group of challenges in field experiments concerns *external validity*—or the ability to transfer impact estimates from the evaluation context to the real-world policy context. *Time horizon effects* can occur when treatment subjects understand that an experimental service is only temporary rather than permanent. *Learning effects* can take place within a community during the course of an evaluation, causing later enrollees to act differently than those enrolled around the time the experiment begins. *Entry effects* not observed during an evaluation can emerge when an appealing service becomes generally available to a population of potential customers, thereby increasing program take-up and system costs. *Hawthorne effects* are responses to treatments that are due not to the content of service but simply to special attention.[3] *Displacement effects*, which may be the most critical external validity concern, occur when treatment-assigned subjects improve their outcomes at the expense of others in the community who are not part of the evaluation sample.[4]

As Zvi Griliches said, "If the data were perfect, collected from well-designed randomized experiments, there would be hardly room for a separate field of econometrics" (Orr 1999, p. 187). The following review mentions few exceptions to the classical assumptions of experimental design and does not delve into any corrections that might have been done before reporting final program impact estimates. The focus here is on average program effects. That is, it focuses on the effect of treatment upon the treated, assuming good experimental designs were properly implemented.

THEORY AND EVIDENCE ON INCENTIVES

Economic theory suggests several reasons why paying UI to unemployed workers might prolong joblessness. Feldstein (1974) argued that moral hazard caused by paying UI leads beneficiaries to exaggerate the involuntary nature of their joblessness so as to prolong unemployment. In a labor-leisure model of choice, UI benefits lower the opportunity cost of deferring reemployment to consume more leisure (O'Leary 1998). In a search model of unemployment, UI raises the reservation wage for accepting a new job, thereby reducing the probability that an acceptable offer arrives in any period (Ehrenberg and Oaxaca 1976). Decker (1997) reviews the econometric literature on UI work disincentives and reports the range of published estimates to be between 0.3 and 1.5 weeks' longer duration of UI receipt for a 10 percentage point increase in the UI replacement rate.

REEMPLOYMENT BONUS EXPERIMENTS

A series of field experiments were conducted to evaluate positive reemployment incentives in UI. Between 1984 and 1989, four reemployment bonus experiments targeted at UI recipients were conducted in the United States. These experiments provided various levels of lump-sum payments to UI recipients who took new, full-time jobs within 6 to 12 weeks of their benefit application and held those jobs for at least three to four months.

The aim was to measure the behavioral response of UI recipients to changes in the timing of benefit payments. The main outcome of interest was to speed return to work in a way that would benefit employees, employers, and the government, and would be cost effective. UI claimants would be better off if they returned to work sooner and found jobs that were similar and paid similar wages to the jobs that they would take in the absence of a bonus offer. Employers would be better off if they had lower UI payroll taxes. The government would be better off if the cost of the bonus were offset by a decrease in UI benefit payments to unemployed workers and an increase in income and other tax contributions by workers during their longer period of employment.

Illinois UI Incentive Experiment

The first bonus experiment was conducted in Illinois during 1984–1985 by the Upjohn Institute and sponsored by the Illinois Department of Employment Security. The design provided a $500 bonus—equal to about four weeks of UI benefits—for reemployment within 11 weeks of applying for benefits if the job was held for four months. The bonus offer was estimated to reduce UI receipt by 1.15 weeks (Woodbury and Spiegelman 1987). Participants suffered no decline in job quality, as reemployment wages did not differ from the prior job, but the estimated cost savings led to a large benefit-cost ratio of 2.32.

New Jersey UI Reemployment Experiment

The U.S. Department of Labor sponsored a New Jersey UI experiment in 1985–1986 that included a reemployment bonus, among other features. The initial bonus offer was one half of the claimant's remaining entitlement at the time of the offer, and it remained constant for the first two full weeks. After that, the bonus offer declined by 10 percent of the original amount each week, falling to zero by the end of the eleventh full week of the bonus offer. Initial bonus offers in New Jersey averaged $1,644, or about nine times the UI weekly benefit amount (Corson et al. 1989). The bonus was estimated to shorten UI durations by about half a week and generated only modest savings in UI.

Pennsylvania and Washington Reemployment Bonus Experiments

In 1987, the Pennsylvania and Washington experiments were designed to test varying bonus offers and search periods. The resulting designs included four treatment groups in Pennsylvania and six in Washington. Each treatment specified a bonus level (high and low in Pennsylvania; high, medium, and low in Washington) and a qualification period or duration of the bonus offer (short and long in both states). The reemployment period of four months was the same for all treatments. Impact estimates on weeks of UI benefits received ranged from −0.04 to −0.84, with a mean effect across the 10 treatments in Pennsylvania and Washington of −0.51 weeks (Decker and O'Leary 1995). The mean estimated savings to the UI program came to $25 per offer.

Targeting Reemployment Bonuses

O'Leary, Decker, and Wandner (2005) investigated whether targeting reemployment bonus offers to unemployment insurance (UI) claimants identified as most likely to exhaust benefits would reduce benefit payments.[5] They showed that targeting bonus offers with profiling models similar to those in state Worker Profiling and Reemployment Services (WPRS) systems can improve cost effectiveness.[6]

However, estimated average benefit payments do not steadily decline, as the eligibility screen for targeting is gradually tightened by the probability of UI exhaustion. They find that narrow targeting is not optimal. The best candidate to emerge is a low bonus amount with a long qualification period, targeted to the half of profiled claimants most likely to exhaust their UI benefit entitlement.

Interpreting Results from the Bonus Experiments

The relatively weak response to the bonus offers in New Jersey, Pennsylvania, and Washington led to a reexamination of the very large Illinois results. It was discovered that within the designed Illinois experiment, a second experiment had unintentionally taken place. In 1984, as Illinois was recovering from a major recession, the availability of Federal Supplemental Compensation (FSC) was terminated. This resulted in about half of the claimants studied having 38 weeks of UI benefit eligibility, with the remainder being eligible for only 26 weeks of regular UI benefits. It turns out that the mean bonus response of −1.15 weeks in Illinois was made up of a response of −1.78 weeks for those eligible for FSC and −0.54 weeks for those not eligible (Davidson and Woodbury 1991). The mean response of −0.54 for the non-FSC sample in Illinois is close to the responses observed in New Jersey, Pennsylvania, and Washington, where the entitled durations of benefits were comparable.

Analysis of treatment impacts by characteristics of participants, industries, and labor markets showed that the reemployment bonus had a remarkably even impact on various subgroups of workers, whether delineated by gender, age, race, industrial sector of employment, level of local unemployment, or level of the weekly benefit amount. The effects of bonus offers did not differ significantly across these important distinctions, suggesting that the bonus offer could be an equitable way to improve program efficiency.

Two potential behavioral effects might reduce cost effectiveness for an operational program (Meyer 1995). First, an actual bonus program could have a displacement effect. Displacement occurs if UI claimants who are offered a bonus increase their rate of reemployment at the expense of other job seekers not offered a bonus. Second, there is also the risk that an operational bonus offer program could induce an *entry effect*. That is, the availability of a reemployment bonus might result in a larger proportion of unemployed job seekers entering the UI system.

If entry and displacement effects are large, actual program cost effectiveness will be smaller. However, targeting offers of a low bonus amount coupled with a long qualification period to only those most likely to exhaust UI could reduce both these risks. Targeting would introduce uncertainty that a bonus offer would be forthcoming upon filing a UI claim, which should reduce the chance of a large entry effect. Also, targeting should reduce any potential for displacement, since a smaller proportion of claimants would receive the bonus offer.[7]

THE UI WORK TEST AND JOB SEARCH ASSISTANCE EXPERIMENTS

Unemployment insurance provides temporary partial wage replacement to the involuntarily unemployed. Proper administration of this objective assures that UI is social insurance and not a dole. Eligibility rules require that UI beneficiaries are strongly attached to the labor force and temporarily jobless through no fault of their own. To initially qualify for UI, a claimant must satisfy both monetary and nonmonetary eligibility requirements. Monetary eligibility for UI is determined by base period earnings.[8] Nonmonetary eligibility rules specify that the job separation must be involuntary. These rules prohibit quits and discharge for causes justifiable by an employer, such as unexplained absences or misconduct. To maintain continuing UI eligibility, beneficiaries also must be able, available, and actively seeking full-time work. Assessment of compliance with the UI work test is normally administered by the ES, which works in cooperation with state UI agencies. An influential audit of UI payment accuracy done for the U.S. Department of Labor reported that a large number of overpayments in the UI system were due to failure to satisfy work search requirements (Burgess and Kingston 1987). This important study spawned a series of evaluations of the UI work test and associated job search requirements.

The UI work test normally involves beneficiaries certifying on their biweekly continued claim form that they have actively searched for work. Most states require beneficiaries to name two or three specific employers contacted about work in the past two weeks. Job search assistance (JSA) comprises a bundle of services available from the public labor exchange, which may include résumé preparation assistance, job finding clubs, provision of labor market information, development of a job search plan, and orientation to self-service resources like job vacancy listings, résumé preparation, word processor competency testing, and telephones for contacting employers. Evaluations of the UI work test and JSA have overlapped.

Four specific evaluations of JSA have been particularly influential in shaping public labor exchange policy. All four were done as field experiments involving random assignment. Among other offerings of the public employment service, job referrals and placements have not applied an experimental design because of the unethical design requirement of withholding from the control group basic services having universal entitlement. Consequently, JSA evaluations have focused on UI claimants and have usually involved providing additional services.

Charleston Claimant Placement and Work Test Experiment

The first field experiment of the UI work test was done in 1983 in Charleston, South Carolina (Corson, Long, and Nicholson 1985). Three treatments represented successively larger bundles of services. The control group was given the customary work test, which involved informing claimants that ES registration was required but involved no systematic monitoring of this requirement. The three treatments involved the following: 1) a strengthened work test, requiring ES registration before a second UI benefit check was paid; 2) added to the first treatment were enhanced placement services, a personal placement interview, a job referral or an outreach attempt to a prospective employer, and training in using the job vacancy listings; 3) in addition to the second treatment, there were special workshops on job search and labor market information.

Impacts of the three treatments on UI weeks were −0.51, −0.61, and −0.76, respectively. Subgroup effects were largest for men (−1.0 weeks) and workers in the construction industry (−4.0 weeks). The biggest marginal benefit came from the first treatment, which relinked ES with UI. Given the low cost per ES participant, all treatments were highly cost effective. The third treatment, which involved the largest number of components, had an average cost per participant of only $17.58 in 1983 dollars.

Washington Alternative Work Search Experiment

An experiment in Tacoma, Washington, conducted between July 1986 and August 1987 tested three differences from the standard work search requirement of three employer contacts per week: 1) elimination of the reporting requirement, 2) individualized stronger work search requirements plus a group eligibility review, and 3) Treatment 2 plus required workshops and additional individual counseling and assistance.

Removing the work test increased UI benefit durations by 3.34 weeks. Treatment 2 did not have a statistically significant effect, but Treatment 3 shortened UI durations by −0.47 weeks (Johnson and Klepinger 1994). An analysis of the timing of responses to the treatments suggested that beneficiaries were more likely to stop UI receipt just before a scheduled intervention, rather than after the service was provided. Such a response might be termed an "invitation effect."

This result raised the question of whether the response was due to the value of the services or the time burden of participation.

Lachowska, Meral, and Woodbury (2015) examined long-term evidence from the Tacoma experiment by merging Washington UI program administrative data from nine additional years after the original one-year follow-up period. They focused on the treatment that removed the work test, and they estimated that nearly all the costs were borne by the UI system in the year of the experimental program change. Long-term effects averaged out to zero, but subgroup analysis by job separation reason yielded an important result for those permanently separated from jobs. For this group, the 10-year follow-up suggested that the standard UI work search requirement yielded significantly faster reemployment and greater long-term employment stability. Those excused from the work test got reemployed about 1.40 calendar quarters later and had job tenure of about 1.65 quarters shorter than the comparison group.

Maryland UI Work Search Experiment

Enrollment in the Maryland UI Work Search Experiment was conducted in six public labor-exchange offices around the state during 1994 (Klepinger et al. 1998). The control group faced the standard work search requirement of reporting two employer contacts per week. The four treatments had the following requirements: 1) reporting of four weekly employer contacts, which did not have to be verified; 2) two weekly employer contacts, which did not have to be reported; 3) reporting of two weekly employer contacts, plus attending a four-day job search workshop; and 4) reporting of two weekly employer contacts—claimants were told contacts would be verified. The treatment impacts on weeks of UI benefits were as follows: −0.7, 0.4, −0.6, and −0.09. Notably, the impact of the fourth treatment occurred during the first spell of joblessness. Similarly, the first treatment generated the bulk of its response during the first spell of joblessness in the benefit year. The effects of Treatments 1, 3, and

4 were not associated with lower reemployment earnings. However, eliminating the work search reporting requirement, as in Treatment 2, raises reemployment earnings by a statistically significant 4 percent.

A second control group facing the standard work test was also tracked, but claimants assigned to this group were told that their behavior was being tracked as part of an experiment. This was done to permit testing for the presence of a Hawthorne effect. This is relevant in ensuring external validity of the evaluation. If part of the treatment response to a new work test is simply due to added attention on the work test, then such an effect could quickly dissipate after actual implementation. Impact estimates computed as a contrast between the participant group and each of the two control groups were virtually identical, suggesting the absence of any Hawthorne effect.[9]

Michigan Reemployment and Eligibility Assessment Nudge

Reemployment and Eligibility Assessments (REAs) involve repeated validation of all aspects of UI eligibility during the benefit year and providing additional reemployment services. In Chapter 4 of this book, Jacob Benus explains the policy development and evaluation results for the REA. The most recent REA evaluation involved random trials in Nevada (Michaelides et al. 2012). The Nevada trials provided evidence that for the REA, both the work test and the reemployment services were separately effective, which is valuable evidence in the face of the Tacoma results.

Michigan received a U.S. Department of Labor grant to deliver REA services in five workforce areas in 2015. The Michigan REA started on January 29, 2015, but only about half of REA-assigned beneficiaries were completing REA. The W.E. Upjohn Institute for Employment Research worked with Mathematica and Ideas42 on a small, randomized controlled trial evaluating a low-cost intervention to increase REA participation in the four-county workforce development area overseen by Michigan Works! Southwest, a One-Stop agency administered by the Upjohn Institute. Random assignment began on March 16, 2015, and ended on September 30, 2015.

In the parlance of behavioral economics, the low-cost interventions were "nudges" for participation (Babcock et al. 2012), as was discussed in Chapter 3. The nudges took the form of a series of e-mails providing information and reminders to participate in REA services. The nudges reminded REA beneficiaries about three required REA appointments. A follow-up set of three "persistence" e-mails were also sent to encourage and reinforce job search activity after the third REA visit to a Michigan Works! office. The persistence e-mails provided links to office locations and phone numbers, schedules of local services, and testimonials from previous service recipients.[10]

The study found that "UI claimants who were sent email messages were more likely to start the REA program by scheduling their first session. UI claimants who received email messages were also more likely to complete the REA program. Once individuals attended their first REA session, they were equally likely to complete the program regardless of whether they had received emails or not" (Darling et al. 2016, p. 1).

TARGETED JOB SEARCH ASSISTANCE

Targeting of JSA surfaced as a policy option during the 1990s, following the massive economic restructuring and worker dislocation of the previous decade. The question of whether JSA would be effective for those at risk of long-term unemployment was evaluated in the New Jersey experiment (Corson et al. 1989). This provided essential evidence to support establishment of the WPRS system, which requires JSA early in the UI benefit year for those most likely to exhaust their UI entitlement (Wandner 1994). Two other experiments evaluated the effectiveness of targeted JSA. The first was done around the time of WPRS start-up (Decker et al. 2000). The other was done in the context of the WPRS program operating in Kentucky (Black et al. 2003).

New Jersey UI Reemployment Experiment

The New Jersey UI Reemployment Experiment ran in 1986 and 1987 (Corson et al. 1989). The sampling frame for random assignment targeted the evaluation to dislocated workers claiming UI benefits by requiring applicants to

1) receive a first UI benefit within five weeks of application,

2) be at least 25 years old,

3) have worked for the pre-UI claim employer at least three years,

4) not be on standby awaiting return to the claimant's previous job with a specific recall date, and

5) not be a union hiring hall member.

The three treatments were as follows: 1) JSA alone, 2) JSA plus an offer of job training,[11] and 3) JSA plus the cash reemployment bonus described above. During the benefit year, weeks of UI benefit receipt declined by −0.47, −0.48, and −0.97 for the three treatments, respectively. All of these impact estimates carried statistical significance. The cumulative impacts on weeks of UI benefit receipt over the six years after the initial benefit claim were −0.76, −0.93, and −1.72 for the three treatments, and the estimated impact from the third treatment was statistically significant (Corson and Haimson 1996). The New Jersey UI Reemployment Experiment demonstrated that JSA targeted to claimants likely to be long-term unemployed had the same cost-effective impact as that found for other groups of UI claimants—about half a week shorter UI receipt.

D.C. and Florida Job Search Assistance Experiment

In 1993, President Clinton signed Public Law 103-152, which required states to establish and use a WPRS system to identify UI claimants most likely to exhaust their regular benefits and provide them with early reemployment services. Under WPRS, UI recipients who are expecting recall or members of a union hall are dropped, because they are not expected to undertake an active independent job search. Then, remaining UI recipients are ranked by their likelihood of exhausting UI benefits. Referrals are then made to early reemployment services in the order of the profiling score until the capacity of local agencies to serve them is exhausted.

The targeted JSA experiment done in Florida and Washington, D.C., in 1995 and 1996 applied what became a standard two-step practice in nearly all states for WPRS: 1) exclude job-attached and union hiring hall members, then 2) evaluate the probability of exhausting UI entitlement and target those with the highest probabilities for the evaluation. From this profiled sample frame, randomization was done to the control group and the three treatments: 1) structured job search assistance orientation, testing, job search workshop, and a one-on-one assessment interview; 2) individualized job search assistance (IJSA) orientation, one-on-one assessment interview, and an individual employability plan; and 3) IJSA+, which is Treatment 2 plus the possibility of job skill training (Decker et al. 2000).

The statistically significant impacts on weeks of UI compensation in the benefit year in Washington, D.C., were -1.13, -0.47, and -0.61, and in Florida they were -0.41, -0.59, and -0.52. There was no evidence of any pre/post wage change, but earnings did rise slightly in the District of Columbia. Structured JSA emerged as the most cost-effective intervention examined.

Kentucky Targeted Reemployment Services

An independent assessment of WPRS in Kentucky based on an experimental design was done by economists at the Center for Business and Economic Research at the University of Kentucky (Black et al. 2003). Kentucky divides the predicted UI exhaustion distribution into 20 ranges. Depending on the level of UI claims, weekly office capacity is reached within one of the 20 groups. Randomization is done on the group margin at capacity—called the tie group. Based on data from 1994 to 1996, the impact estimates for WPRS in Kentucky were −2.2 weeks of UI, −$143 in UI benefits, and a $1,054 increase in earnings during the UI benefit year. The difference in these estimates from the national WPRS evaluation was most likely due to the fact that Black et al. essentially confined their contrasts within profiling tie groups, thereby achieving a closer counterfactual. The authors noted that the reduced duration was mainly due to no-shows for the profiling services, but it may be the case that these UI beneficiaries simply returned to work earlier.

The extraordinary foresight of the Kentucky Department of Employment Services to include randomization in assignment to WPRS should be a model for all state and local employment-service delivery agencies. In setting up WPRS administrative rules, the Kentucky agency realized the value of evaluation research and used that orientation to help resolve the resource allocation problem. When resources are limited, randomization in program assignment can always be viewed as an equitable mechanism. It has the added benefit of providing for strong evaluation evidence.

EMPLOYER INCENTIVES

Most public employment programs focus on the supply side of the labor market. Evaluations have also been done of interventions to increase labor demand. This section reviews field experiments done to induce hiring, self-employment, or job retention.

Illinois UI Hiring Incentive Experiment

Another experiment tested an intervention that amounted to a wage subsidy that was not restricted to economically disadvantaged workers but may have stigmatized job seekers. Woodbury and Spiegelman (1987) report that for the Illinois Reemployment Bonus

Experiment, cash bonuses paid directly to persons who gain reemployment have a powerful effect in reducing the duration of unemployment, whereas if a cash payment for hiring a job seeker is made to employers, the effect is almost nil. Employers may be reluctant to hire workers who present a voucher for payment from the state because it signals that the worker may have "hidden" characteristics that hinder their finding employment without a state subsidy. Most programs for the unemployed are either income-support or labor-supply enhancing; the wage subsidy is a labor-demand stimulus. But apparently regardless of the form of delivery of the subsidy to employers, it has a stigmatizing effect on workers. An obvious alternative is the wage supplement, which is paid directly to workers. This type of program has even been recommended to help welfare recipients (who might face the most severe stigma) gain reemployment.[12]

Dayton Wage Subsidy Experiment

Not specifically in the context of UI, but germane to stimulating employer hiring, a targeted wage subsidy was operated as a field experiment with random trials in 1980–1981 by the U.S. Department of Labor in Dayton, Ohio. The evaluation involved two treatments: 1) a hiring tax credit and 2) a lump-sum cash subsidy payment, plus a control group of otherwise similar employers. Burtless (1985, p. 106) writes that "the results show conclusively that workers known to be eligible for targeted wage subsidies were significantly less likely to find jobs than were otherwise identical workers whose eligibility for subsidies was not advertised." Burtless (1985, p. 105) speculates that "the vouchers had a stigmatizing effect and provided a screening device with which employers discriminated against economically disadvantaged workers."

Self-Employment Experiments

Self-employment programs for unemployed persons have been operating in Europe since 1979.[13] Seventeen countries belonging to the Organisation for Economic Co-operation and Development have programs patterned after either the French model, which grants a lump sum payment, or the British model, which provides a series of periodic support payments during the start-up phase of self-employment.[14] The British model amounts to a waiver of the work search requirements for continued receipt of periodic UI payments. American experiments tested the French model in Washington State and the British model in Massachusetts (Benus et al. 1995).

The Massachusetts self-employment experiment ran from 1990 to 1993 and provided UI payments every two weeks for up to 30 weeks. The treatment group increased self-employment, reduced the length of unemployment, increased earnings, and increased recipients' total time in employment—including self-employment plus wage and salary employment. The treatment was cost effective for project participants, society as a whole, and the government sector as well. Total earnings of the average project participant increased by $5,940 over the amount earned by the average control-group member over the three-year follow-up period.

The Washington UI Self-Employment and Enterprise Demonstration (SEED) enrolled UI beneficiaries from 1989 to 1990, with business services available for participants through March 1991. The SEED lump sum payment was the remainder of a UI beneficiary's entitlement at the start of self-employment. Only about 4 percent of targeted Washington UI claimants met the initial eligibility requirements of attending an orientation and submitting an application. Compared to the control group, treatments spent about four months more in self-employment, earned more from self-employment, spent about one month less in wage and salary employment, had higher rates of employment, reduced the length of the first unemployment spell, and had higher total UI payments during the benefit year (including the lump sum payment).

The periodic payment model as tested in Massachusetts became a UI policy option for states to provide self-employment assistance (SEA) under the North American Free Trade Agreement in 1993.

In 1998, SEA became a permanent UI feature under the Workforce Investment Act of 1998. Eleven states quickly authorized SEA programs. Currently the program is actively used in Delaware, Mississippi, New Hampshire, New York, and Oregon.

Work Sharing Experiments

Work sharing under UI is commonly known as short-time compensation (STC).[15] Under STC, work reductions are shared among employees by reducing work hours instead of putting some workers on layoff. The STC program partially replaces lost earnings by paying a percentage of the full UI weekly benefit amount equal to the percentage reduction in weekly work hours. The STC program is not widely used. A field experiment was conducted in Iowa and Oregon in 2015 and 2016 to test whether informational efforts could increase employer STC program awareness and program use (Houseman et al. 2017).

In Iowa and in the Portland, Oregon, metropolitan area, researchers constructed stratified samples of all employers and randomly assigned them to treatment and control groups to test informational efforts sent by postal mail. In Oregon outside the Portland metro area, Oregon Worksource Regions were divided into "treatment" and "comparison" regions, and group informational sessions and regionalized advertising efforts were made in addition to mailings.[16]

Use of STC by Iowa employers did not change appreciably after the interventions began. However, the pattern of weekly STC payments in Iowa suggested that employers tried to take advantage of temporary federal payment of STC benefits, and results from employer surveys suggested a statistically significant increase in awareness about STC in the Iowa treatment group.[17] In Oregon, there was also statistically significant evidence that informational efforts had a positive effect on employer awareness about STC. Furthermore, Oregon treatment employers started significantly more STC plans in both trials, with a 58 percent difference in the RCT and a 100 percent difference in the quasi-experimental design (Houseman et al. 2017).

The experiments in Iowa and Oregon showed that informational outreach can increase employer use of STC. Currently, 28 states have STC plans, and in those states, STC is used relatively infrequently compared to regular UI (Balducchi 2015). If STC were available in all states, in recession periods STC could be used as a channel for fiscal policy by supplementing emergency federal extended unemployment benefits.

SUMMARY AND RELEVANCE TO UI TODAY

As social insurance, UI partially replaces lost income for labor force members who are involuntarily separated from their jobs and actively seeking work. The program embodies elements of both private insurance and social assistance. While benefit levels are related to prior earnings, they do not completely replace lost earnings but pay an amount that is directly related to prior wage levels up to a socially determined adequate weekly maximum. The elements most reflecting private insurance principles involve testing initial and continuing eligibility for benefits by work search requirements.

Research in the 1970s recognized the moral hazard risks of work disincentives resulting from paying UI benefits and estimated the effects to be between 0.5 and 1.5 weeks for a 10 percent increase in the wage replacement rate. This work led to a series of UI-related field experiments to identify improved administrative practices and incentives to control system costs and improve beneficiary outcomes. The reemployment bonus experiments in the 1980s estimated that offers would reduce UI durations by an average of 0.5 weeks and be modestly cost effective. Simulations based on the bonus experiments found that a bonus amount smaller than the average, when targeted to the half of UI-eligible beneficiaries who are most likely to exhaust UI, achieved a 0.5-week reduction more cost effectively. Field experiments estimating the effects of strengthening work search requirements estimated UI duration reductions of between 0.5 and 1.0

week. An experiment removing the work test saw durations jump by 3.3 weeks. The UI work test involves connecting the unemployed to job search assistance. Experimental evaluations of targeted job search assistance estimated UI durations to be shortened by between 0.5 and 2.2 weeks.

Field experiments evaluating hiring incentives offered to employers have generally not been found to be cost-effective policy options, mainly because of low employer take-up. However, some smaller UI programs show promise as labor demand policies—particularly when properly targeted. Field experiments that paid UI as self-employment assistance with a work search waiver during the business start-up phase, and targeted to those most likely to exhaust UI, were found to be cost neutral to the UI system and often led to second-order employment effects through hiring. Work sharing, or short-time compensation (STC), which pays employees a fraction of their weekly UI equal to the proportionate reduction in work hours, can help employers control layoff costs and retain talent during business downturns. A recent field experiment suggests that employers will sometimes use STC instead of layoffs when they know how STC works.

The federal-state UI program is now gradually rebuilding system reserves after the Great Recession. Many states were left with billions in debt from paying regular benefits, even though the federal government fully paid for benefit extensions at unprecedented levels. Some states are retreating from accepted standards of UI adequacy with the expectation that the federal government will once again intervene when a new unemployment crisis emerges.[18] However, after welfare reform, all social policy is now employment policy. Making and maintaining connections to the workforce is the only path to self-sufficiency. Policymakers are looking for improvements to the public employment system that will be cost effective, or at least cost neutral. There is no silver bullet that will fix everything at once. The experiments reviewed in this chapter offer a practical menu of choices to rebuild an employment security system that is a stronger part of the social safety net for all Americans.

Notes

1. Heckman, Lalonde, and Smith (1999) enumerate the assumptions implicit in such a view of random-assignment field experiments as a means for model-free impact estimation.
2. When there is nonrandom assignment to either a program participant group or the comparison group, proper estimation of program impacts requires statistical methods of correction. See O'Leary (2017).
3. A Hawthorne effect is the initial improvement in a process of production caused by the obtrusive observation of that process. The effect was first noticed in the Hawthorne Works plant of the Western Electric Co. in Cicero, Illinois, during studies of workplace behavior in the 1920s and '30s. Production increased not as a result of actual changes in working conditions introduced by the plant's management but because management demonstrated interest in such improvements. A reexamination of the Hawthorne data has called into question whether such an effect actually occurred during the original studies (Jones 1992).
4. This discussion of impact estimation and most of the studies reviewed here focus on partial equilibrium effects of interventions. That is, they assume away external validity issues that include general equilibrium effects such as entry and displacement effects. Some evaluations have directly measured these effects (Davidson and Woodbury 1993).
5. Targeted reemployment bonuses were also tested in a field experiment (Wandner 2012) as part of personal reemployment accounts (PRAs). However, the design of the bonus offers under PRAs was not similar to the earlier experiments, and the bonus take-up was low among UI beneficiaries who accepted a PRA offer. Furthermore, across the seven states where targeted PRAs were tried, only 45 percent of PRA money was paid out in reemployment bonuses. An even larger share of PRA money was paid for supportive services (Kirby et al. 2008).
6. More on WPRS is in the section on targeted job search assistance.
7. Davidson and Woodbury (1993) estimate that a nontargeted bonus offer to all UI claimants could increase unemployment durations among those not eligible for UI by between 0.2 and 0.4 weeks.
8. The UI base period is normally the first four of the previous five completed calendar quarters before the date of claim for benefits. For UI claimants not eligible based on earnings in the standard base period, earnings in an alternate base year—the four most recently completed calendar quarters—are considered for monetary eligibility in 41 states.
9. A 1987 employment service reform in the United Kingdom called "Restart" was evaluated by Dolton and O'Neill (1996, 2002). They

found evidence that, over the short term, required JSA may appear to act as a stick, prodding UC beneficiaries back to work, but over the long term an earlier JSA intervention supports higher success in the labor market and higher earnings—evidence that JSA can have valuable content for job seekers.

10. Only one recipient of a persistence nudge e-mail opted out of the reminder and reinforcement service.
11. Treatment 2 also had a relocation allowance, but it was rarely used.
12. See for example Lerman (1985).
13. Background information on the European experience with and the American experiments in self-employment for unemployed persons can be found in Wandner (1994).
14. The French model is followed in Luxembourg, Norway, Portugal, Spain, and Sweden; the British model in Australia, Belgium, Canada, Denmark, Finland, Greece, Ireland, Italy, Netherlands, and Germany.
15. In Germany, where it is widely used, the program is known as *kurzarbeit*, meaning "short-work."
16. Following Bloom (2000), the minimum detectable effect in the Oregon quasi-experimental design (QED) evaluation will be larger than in the RCT evaluation by a factor approximated by the square root of $[1/(1 - R^2_A)]$, where R^2_A is the coefficient of determination from the regression of the QED treatment indicator on characteristics of employers in the treatment and control samples.
17. The Middle Class Tax Relief and Job Creation Act of 2012 relieved STC employers of UI benefit charges by reimbursing states so employer UI tax rates would not increase (O'Leary, forthcoming).
18. The potential duration of regular UI benefits is no longer at least 26 weeks in all states.

References

Babcock, Linda, William J. Congdon, Lawrence F. Katz, and Sendhil Mullainathan. 2012. "Notes on Behavioral Economics and Labor Market Policy." *IZA Journal of Labor Policy* 1(2): 1–14.

Balducchi, David E. 2015. "Selling Work Sharing in Virginia: Lessons from the Campaign to Enact Short-Time Compensation, 2011–2014." In *Transforming U.S. Workforce Development Policies for the 21st Century*, Carl Van Horn, Tammy Edwards, and Todd Greene, eds. Kalamazoo, MI: W.E. Upjohn Institute for Employment Research, pp. 543–559.

Benus, Jacob M., Terry R. Johnson, Michelle Wood, Neelima Grover, and Theodore Shen. 1995. "Self-Employment Programs: A New Reemployment Strategy—Final Report on the UI Self-Employment Demonstration." Unemployment Insurance Occasional Paper No. 954. Washington, DC: U.S. Department of Labor.

Black, Dan, Jeffrey Smith, Mark Berger, and Brett Noel. 2003. "Is the Threat of Reemployment Services More Effective than the Services Themselves? Evidence from Random Assignment in the UI System." *American Economic Review* 93(4): 1313–1327.

Bloom, Howard. 2000. "Sample Size and Allocation for Randomized Experiments." Lecture notes for Evaluation Workshop Session No. 1 of Day 2, February 3, 2000. New York: Manpower Demonstration Research Corporation (MDRC).

Burgess, Paul L., and Jerry L. Kingston. 1987. *An Incentives Approach to Improving the Unemployment Compensation System.* Kalamazoo, MI: W.E. Upjohn Institute for Employment Research.

Burtless, Gary. 1985. "Are Targeted Wage Subsidies Harmful? Evidence from a Wage Voucher Experiment." *Industrial and Labor Relations Review* 39(1): 105–114.

Corson, Walter, Paul T. Decker, Sherri M. Dunstan, Anne R. Gordon, Patricia Anderson, and John Homrighausen. 1989. "New Jersey Unemployment Insurance Reemployment Demonstration Project." Unemployment Insurance Occasional Paper No. 89-3. Washington, DC: U.S. Department of Labor, Employment and Training Administration.

Corson, Walter, and Joshua Haimson. 1996. "The New Jersey Unemployment Insurance Reemployment Demonstration Project Six-Year Follow-Up and Summary Report." UI Occasional Paper No. 96-2. Washington, DC: U.S. Department of Labor, Employment and Training Administration.

Corson, Walter, David Long, and Walter Nicholson. 1985. "Evaluation of the Charleston Claimant Placement and Work Test Demonstration." Unemployment Insurance Occasional Paper No. 85-2. Washington, DC: U.S. Department of Labor, Employment and Training Administration.

Darling, Matthew, Christopher J. O'Leary, Irma Perez-Johnson, Jaclyn Lefkowitz, Ken Kline, Ben Damerow, and Randall W. Eberts. 2016. "Encouragement Emails Increase Participation in Reemployment Services." DOL Behavioral Interventions Project Brief. Washington, DC: U.S. Department of Labor, Chief Evaluation Officer.

Davidson, Carl, and Stephen A. Woodbury. 1991. "Effects of a Reemployment Bonus under Differing Benefit Entitlements, or, Why the Illinois Experiment Worked." Unpublished manuscript. East Lansing, MI: Michigan State University.

———. 1993. "The Displacement Effect of Reemployment Bonus Programs." *Journal of Labor Economics* 11(4): 575–605.

Decker, Paul T. 1997. "Work Incentives and Disincentives." In *Unemploy-

ment Insurance in the United States: Analysis of Policy Issues, Christopher J. O'Leary and Stephen A. Wandner, eds. Kalamazoo, MI: W.E. Upjohn Institute for Employment Research, pp. 285–320.

Decker, Paul T., and Christopher J. O'Leary. 1995. "Evaluating Pooled Evidence from the Reemployment Bonus Experiments." *Journal of Human Resources* 30(3): 534–550.

Decker, Paul T., Robert B. Olson, Lance Freeman, and Daniel H. Klepinger. 2000. "Assisting Unemployment Insurance Claimants: The Long-Term Impact of the Job Search Assistance Demonstration." OWS Occasional Paper No. 2000-02. Washington, DC: U.S. Department of Labor.

Dolton, Peter, and Donal O'Neill. 1996. "Unemployment Duration and the Restart Effect." *Economic Journal* 106(2): 387–400.

———. 2002. "The Long-Run Effects of Unemployment Monitoring and Work-Search Programs: Experimental Evidence from the United Kingdom." *Journal of Labor Economics* 20(2, Part 1): 381–403.

Ehrenberg, Ronald G., and Ronald Oaxaca. 1976. "Unemployment Insurance, Duration of Unemployment, and Subsequent Wage Gain." *American Economic Review* 66(5): 754–766.

Feldstein, Martin S. 1974. "Unemployment Compensation: Adverse Incentives and Distributional Anomalies." *National Tax Journal* 27(2): 231–244.

Heckman, James J., Neil Hohmann, Jeffrey Smith, and Michael Khoo. 2000. "Substitution and Dropout Bias in Social Experiments: A Study of an Influential Social Experiment." *Quarterly Journal of Economics* 115(2): 651–694.

Heckman, James J., Robert J. LaLonde, and Jeffrey A. Smith. 1999. "The Economics and Econometrics of Active Labor Market Programs." In *Handbook of Labor Economics,* Vol. 3A, Orley Ashenfelter and David Card, eds. Amsterdam: Elsevier, pp. 1865–2097.

Houseman, Susan, Frank Bennici, Susan Labin, Katharine Abraham, Chris O'Leary, and Richard Sigman. 2017. *Demonstration and Evaluation of the Short-Time Compensation Program in Iowa and Oregon: Final Report.* Rockville, MD: Westat.

Johnson, Terry R., and Daniel H. Klepinger. 1994. "Experimental Evidence on Unemployment Insurance Work-Search Policies." *Journal of Human Resources* 29(3): 695–717.

Jones, Stephen R. G. 1992. "Was There a Hawthorne Effect?" *American Journal of Sociology* 98(3): 451–468.

Kirby, Gretchen, Margaret Sullivan, Elizabeth Potamites, Jackie Kauff, Elizabeth Clary, and Charles McGlew. 2008. "Responses to Personal Reemployment Accounts (PRAs): Findings from the Demonstration States—Final Evaluation Report." ETA Occasional Paper No. 2008-07. Washington, DC: U.S. Department of Labor.

110 O'Leary

Klepinger, Daniel H., Terry R. Johnson, Jutta. M. Joesch, Jacob M. Benus. 1998. "Evaluation of the Maryland Unemployment Insurance Work Search Demonstration." Unemployment Insurance Occasional Paper No. 98-2. Washington, DC: U.S. Department of Labor.

Lachowska, Marta, Merve Meral, and Stephen A. Woodbury. 2015. "The Effects of Eliminating the Work Search Requirement on Job Match Quality and Other Long-Term Employment Outcomes." Washington, DC: U.S. Department of Labor.

Lerman, Robert I. 1985. "Separating Income Support from Income Supplementation." *Journal of the Institute for Socioeconomic Studies* 10(Autumn): 101–125.

Meyer, Bruce D. 1995. "Lessons from the U.S. Unemployment Insurance Experiments." *Journal of Economic Literature* 33(1): 91–131.

Michaelides, Marios, Eileen Poe-Yamagata, Jacob Benus, and Dharmendra Tirumalasetti. 2012. "Impact of the Reemployment and Eligibility Assessment (REA) Initiative in Nevada." Employment and Training Occasional Paper No. 2012-08. Washington, DC: U.S. Department of Labor.

O'Leary, Christopher J. 1998. "The Adequacy of Unemployment Insurance Benefits." In *Research in Employment Policy*. Vol. 1, *Reform of the Unemployment Insurance System*, Laurie J. Bassi and Stephen A. Woodbury, eds. Stamford, CT: JAI Press, pp. 63–110.

———. 2017. "Evaluating Public Employment Programs with Field Experiments: A Survey of American Evidence." Upjohn Institute Working Paper No. 17-279. Kalamazoo, MI: W.E. Upjohn Institute for Employment Research.

O'Leary, Christopher J., Paul T. Decker, and Stephen A. Wandner. 2005. "Cost Effectiveness of Targeted Reemployment Bonuses." *Journal of Human Resources* 40(1): 270–279.

Orr, Larry L. 1999. *Social Experiments*. Thousand Oaks, CA: Sage.

Wandner, Stephen A., ed. 1994. "The Worker Profiling and Reemployment Services System: Legislation, Implementation Process, and Research Findings." UI Occasional Paper No. 94-4. Washington, DC: U.S. Department of Labor, Employment and Training Administration.

———. 2012. *Personal Reemployment Accounts: Mitt Romney's Training Voucher and Reemployment Bonus Proposal*. Washington, DC: Urban Institute.

Woodbury, Stephen A., and Robert G. Spiegelman. 1987. "Bonuses to Workers and Employers to Reduce Unemployment: Randomized Trials in Illinois." *American Economic Review* 77(4): 513–530.

Authors

Samia Amin is director of the Workforce Development Practice Area at the American Institutes for Research. In the past she worked as a senior researcher for Mathematica Policy Research, where she was an evaluation design specialist; she has also held positions at the World Bank, the Center for International Development at Harvard University, and the Carnegie Endowment for International Peace. Her focus is on workforce development, self-employment assistance, job training, and international development programs. She has a master's degree in political economy and development from Harvard's Kennedy School of Government.

Jacob M. Benus is cofounder of IMPAQ International, where he serves as executive vice president and director of research. He has more than 30 years of experience in designing and implementing research and evaluation projects for domestic and international economic development and workforce programs; his particular focus is unemployment insurance and other employment and training programs, having led projects in the Czech Republic, China, South Africa, Honduras, Peru, Jordan, Turkey, Armenia, Romania, and Bosnia and Herzegovina. Before founding IMPAQ, he served as project director at the Stanford Research Institute (now SRI International) and manager of the International Safety Net Group at Abt Associates. He earned a PhD in economics from the University of Michigan.

Randall W. Eberts is president of the W.E. Upjohn Institute for Employment Research. His research focuses on the public workforce development system, with particular emphasis on statistical methodologies to set performance targets, determinants of student achievement, and factors related to local and regional economic development. Recently, he has worked with the U.S. Department of Labor to develop and implement a framework for adjusting local, state, and national performance targets for the workforce system. He served as senior staff economist on the President's Council of Economic Advisers and assistant vice president and economist at the Federal Reserve Bank of Cleveland. He earned a PhD in economics from Northwestern University.

Annalisa Mastri is a senior researcher at Mathematica Policy Research. Her areas of expertise include evaluation design, systematic reviews, workforce development programs, and TANF. She led the analysis of administrative data and the benefit-cost analysis for Mathematica's random-assignment evaluation of the Workforce Investment Act's Adult and Dislocated Worker Programs and is principal investigator for the U.S. Department of Labor's

Clearinghouse for Labor Evaluation and Research. She earned a PhD in education economics from Stanford University.

Christopher J. O'Leary is a senior economist at the W.E. Upjohn Institute for Employment Research. His research aims to identify ways of improving public employment policies, including both unemployment insurance and active labor market programs. In particular, his work in unemployment insurance has examined experience rating, benefit adequacy, profiling, and personal reemployment accounts. Through field experiments he has studied UI programs for reemployment bonuses, partial benefits, and work sharing. In Canada, China, Hungary, Poland, and Serbia, he has done impact evaluations and performance monitoring systems for job training, wage subsidies, self-employment assistance, and public service employment. He earned his PhD in economics from the University of Arizona.

Irma Perez-Johnson is vice president for research and evaluation at American Institutes for Research (AIR). Before that, she served as associate director of human services research in Mathematica Policy Research's Princeton, New Jersey, office. Her expertise is in design and implementation of rigorous evaluations of employment training and K–12 education programs, including pilots and demonstrations. For the U.S. Department of Education, she currently leads the evaluation of the Self-Employment Training Demonstration and directs the study of Behavioral Interventions for Labor-Related Programs, and she served as project director and principal investigator for the Evaluation of the Individual Training Account Experiment. She holds a PhD in education policy and evaluation from the University of Pennsylvania.

Stephen A. Wandner is a research fellow at the W.E. Upjohn Institute and a visiting fellow at the Urban Institute. Formerly he directed strategic planning for the Employment and Training Administration (ETA) of the U.S. Department of Labor. Before that he was director of research for the ETA, and earlier he held the same position for the Unemployment Insurance Service. In both cases, he conducted and directed research on labor issues, including eight Unemployment Insurance Experiments, all dealing with dislocated workers. He has coedited three previous books for the Upjohn Institute: *Unemployment Insurance in the United States* (1997) with Christopher J. O'Leary; *Targeting Employment Services* (2002), with Randall W. Eberts and O'Leary; and *Job Training Policy in the United States* (2004), with O'Leary and Robert A. Straits; and he wrote *Solving the Reemployment Puzzle: From Research to Policy* (Upjohn Institute 2010). He earned his PhD in economics from Indiana University.

Index

Note: The italic letters *b, f, n,* and *t* following a page number indicate a box, figure, note, or table, respectively, on that page. Double letters refer to more than one such item on that page.

Layoffs *vs.* STC use, 105
Lessons learned from public workforce
    experiments
    compensating service providers with
        incentives, 20, 22, 23, 30, 38
    conducting RCT, 4–8, 41–42
    considering design, implementation,
        and evaluation, 7, 8–9, 13–39
    developing resources to support
        implementation, 26–27, 38
    documenting variation in program
        implementation, 31–33, 39
    enrolling states or localities as
        participants, 5–6, 21–22, 37–38
    minimizing burden on local staff,
        23–27, 29–31, 38
    monitoring experiments, 6–7, 27–29,
        28*b*, 33–34
    securing funds for research, 4–5, 23,
        37, 38
    using results, 8, 10
Local workforce agencies, 43
    recruitment of, as service providers,
        5–6, 46–48
Local Workforce Investment Areas
    (LWIAs)
    participant *vs.* nonparticipant, in
        study design, 21, 22
    random assignment to ITA
        experiments in, 15, 16
    SET demonstration and, 26–27, 28*b*,
        29, 33–34
    Work First pilot and, 56–57
Local Workforce Investment Boards
    (LWIBs), 57
    culture of, 47, 56–57
    low-cost RCT and, 42–43, 43–44, 48,
        56
    responsibility of, and USDOL
        negotiations, 46, 47, 57
    support of state agencies needed by,
        47–48
Luxembourg, French SEA model used in,
    102, 107*n*14
LWIAs. *See* Local Workforce Investment
    Areas
LWIBs. *See* Local Workforce Investment
    Boards

Manpower Demonstration Research
    Corporation (MDRC), research
    evaluation by, 7
Maryland, UI work search experiments
    in, 10, 65, 95–96
Massachusetts, 10
    SEA in, 8, 102
    social intervention experiments in, 5,
        11*n*5
Mathematica Policy Research, 58*n*3
    low-cost RCT evaluation by, 96–97
    research evaluation by, 7, 9, 14–17
Michigan
    Kalamazoo–St. Joseph Workforce
        Development Board in, 50, 57
    REA nudge experiment, 10, 96–97,
        107*n*10
    USDOL funding of, projects, 3, 10,
        58*n*3, 96
    Work First Experiment in, 8, 50–56
Michigan Works! Southwest, as One-
    Stop agency, 96–97
Middle Class Tax Relief and Job
    Creation Act (2012), STC
    employers and, 107*n*17
Minnesota, REA initiative implemented
    in, 70–71
Mississippi, SEA as NAFTA option used
    in, 103
Moral hazard, UI benefits receipt and,
    88, 104
Murray, Senator Patti, bipartisanship
    of, 3

National Directory of New Hires, as
    wage-record work-around, 6
National Worker Profiling and
    Reemployment Service
    evaluation, duration of UI
    benefits and, 66
Netherlands, British SEA model used in,
    102, 107*n*14
Nevada REA initiative
    effect of, 8, 9–10
    evaluation of, 76–79
    impact results of, 75–76, 96
    as model for RESEA, 79, 80, 81

About the Institute

The W.E. Upjohn Institute for Employment Research is a nonprofit research organization devoted to finding and promoting solutions to employment-related problems at the national, state, and local levels. It is an activity of the W.E. Upjohn Unemployment Trustee Corporation, which was established in 1932 to administer a fund set aside by Dr. W.E. Upjohn, founder of The Upjohn Company, to seek ways to counteract the loss of employment income during economic downturns.

The Institute is funded largely by income from the W.E. Upjohn Unemployment Trust, supplemented by outside grants, contracts, and sales of publications. Activities of the Institute comprise the following elements: 1) a research program conducted by a resident staff of professional social scientists; 2) a competitive grant program, which expands and complements the internal research program by providing financial support to researchers outside the Institute; 3) a publications program, which provides the major vehicle for disseminating the research of staff and grantees, as well as other selected works in the field; and 4) an Employment Management Services division, which manages most of the publicly funded employment and training programs in the local area.

The broad objectives of the Institute's research, grant, and publication programs are to 1) promote scholarship and experimentation on issues of public and private employment and unemployment policy, and 2) make knowledge and scholarship relevant and useful to policymakers in their pursuit of solutions to employment and unemployment problems.

Current areas of concentration for these programs include causes, consequences, and measures to alleviate unemployment; social insurance and income maintenance programs; compensation; workforce quality; work arrangements; family labor issues; labor-management relations; and regional economic development and local labor markets.

CPSIA information can be obtained
at www.ICGtesting.com
Printed in the USA
FFOW05n0901101117